CANADA

Symbols of Nationhood

"… Canada is a country that has been blessed beyond most countries in the world. It is a country worth working for."

Queen Elizabeth II,
Canada Day Celebrations on Parliament Hill,
Ottawa, July 1, 1990.

Symbols and the story of Canada

Every country has its own set of symbols that establish its identity and set it apart from other countries of the world. Symbols tell the story of a nation, its people, environment and history. They represent values, goals and aspirations shared by all its citizens.

Canada is a land of diversity, embracing vast differences within its borders and among its people. For Canadians, symbols provide connections across space and time and are a source of unity and pride.

Canadian symbols are as diverse as Canada's history. The beaver tells of the importance of the fur trade, the maple tree tells of the early settlers and the magnificence of our forests. The fleur-de-lis is symbolic of France, one of the founding countries of Canada. The Union Jack, still prominent in Canada, shows our strong links with the United Kingdom.

Canada's symbols tell of a country made up of many different peoples. This story includes the Indians and Inuit who lived in Canada long before recorded history; the French and English who were the first Europeans to establish permanent settlements in Canada; and the people from many other nations who settled this great land and are proud to call themselves Canadians.

Our wilderness is predominant in our symbols and reflects the importance of nature to our Canadian identity. Our abundance of animals and forests, lakes and rivers makes Canada special. We value our natural heritage as we value our people.

Contents

Canada

Origin of the name

The name Canada comes from the Huron-Iroquois word "kanata", meaning village or settlement. In 1535, two Indian youths told French explorer Jacques Cartier about the route to "kanata" (the site of present-day Quebec City). Cartier used the word "Canada" to describe not only the village but the entire area controlled by its chief. The name was soon applied to a much larger area: maps in 1547 designated everything north of the St. Lawrence River as "Canada".

Cartier also called the St. Lawrence River the "rivière du Canada", a name used until the early 1600s. By 1616, although the entire region was known as New France, the area along the great river of Canada and the Gulf of St. Lawrence was still called Canada.

OTTAWA

Population (1999) . . .30,553,000
Area: Land . . . . . .9,215,430 km²
Fresh water . . . . . . .755,180 km²
Total . . . . .9,970,610 km²
Capital . . . . .Ottawa
Date of Confederation —
July 1, 1867

Soon explorers and fur traders opened up territory to the west and to the south and the area known as "Canada" grew. In the early 1700s, the name referred to all lands in what is now the American mid-west and as far south as present-day Louisiana.

The first use of "Canada" as an official name came in 1791 when the Province of Quebec was divided into the colonies of Upper and Lower Canada. In 1841, the two Canadas were united under one name, the Province of Canada. At Confederation, in 1867, the new country assumed the name "Canada" under Section 3 of the *Constitution Act, 1867*.

History

Today, Canada is made up of ten provinces and three territories.

However, in 1867, when the *British North America Act*, 1867 created the

new Dominion of Canada, there were only four provinces — Ontario, Quebec, Nova Scotia and New Brunswick.

Three years after Confederation, Canada purchased Rupert's Land from the Hudson's Bay Company, which had been granted a charter to the area by the British government exactly two centuries earlier. Rupert's Land spanned all land drained by rivers flowing into Hudson's Bay — roughly 40 percent of present-day Canada. The selling price was 300,000 pounds sterling.

Also in 1870, Britain transferred the North-Western Territory to Canada. Previously, the Hudson's Bay Company had an exclusive licence to trade in this area, which stretched west to the colony of British Columbia and north to the Arctic Circle. When it was discovered in the mid-1800s that the prairies had enormous farming potential, the British government refused to renew the company's licence. With the Hudson's Bay Company out of the area, Britain was free to turn it over to Canada.

Rupert's Land and the North-Western Territory were combined to form the Northwest Territories. The *Manitoba Act* of 1870 created the province of Manitoba from a small part of this area.

Maple Leaf

In 1871, British Columbia joined the union with the promise of a railway to link it to the rest of the country.

In 1873, Prince Edward Island, which had previously declined an offer to join Confederation, became Canada's seventh province.

Yukon, which had been a district of the Northwest Territories since 1895, became a separate territory in 1898.

Meanwhile, Canada was opening up its west, just as its neighbour to the south had done before. Migrants

Maple Tree

from eastern Canada and immigrants from Europe began to fill the prairies, which were still part of the Northwest Territories. Then, in 1905, the provinces of Saskatchewan and Alberta were created, completing the map of Western Canada.

After great debate and two referenda, the people of Newfoundland and Labrador voted to join Confederation in 1949, creating Canada's tenth province.

On April 1, 1999, Nunavut, covering 1.9 million square kilometres of Canada's eastern Arctic, was created from the eastern part of the Northwest Territories.

Coat of Arms

The arms of Canada were adopted in 1921 by proclamation of King George V. In 1994, the arms were augmented with a ribbon displaying the motto of the Order of Canada, DESIDERANTES MELIOREM PATRIAM (They desire a better country).

The design of the arms of Canada reflects the royal symbols of the United Kingdom and France (the three royal lions of England, the royal lion of Scotland, the royal fleurs-de-lis of France and the royal Irish harp of Tara). On the bottom portion of the shield is a sprig of three Canadian maple leaves representative of Canadians of all origins. The coat of arms is supported by the lion of England holding the Royal Union Flag and the unicorn of Scotland carrying the flag of Royal France. The crest above the shield features a crowned lion holding a red maple leaf. At the base of the arms are the floral emblems associated with the Canadian Monarchy: the English rose, the Scottish thistle, the French fleur-de-lis and the Irish shamrock.

Motto

A MARI USQUE AD MARE
(From sea to sea)

Flag

The national flag of Canada was adopted by resolutions of the House of Commons and Senate in 1964 and proclaimed by Queen Elizabeth ll to take effect on February 15, 1965. The anniversary of this event is observed every February 15 as National Flag of Canada Day across the country.

The adoption of the national flag of Canada was the culmination of many years of discussion, hundreds of designs and a heated debate in Parliament. The search for a new Canadian flag began in 1925 when a Committee of the Privy Council began to investigate potential designs. In 1946, a parliamentary committee examined more than 2,600 submissions but could not reach agreement on a new design. As the centennial of Confederation approached, Parliament increased its efforts to choose a new flag. On February 15, 1965, the national flag of Canada was raised for the first time over Parliament Hill.

The flag is red and white, the official colours of Canada, with a stylized eleven-point maple leaf at its centre. The flag's proportions are two by length and one by width.

National Sports

By an Act assented to on May 12, 1994, the Parliament of Canada has declared ice hockey as the national winter sport of Canada and lacrosse as Canada's national summer sport.

Canada

THE CROWN IN CANADA — I

The Queen's Personal Canadian Flag

In 1962, Queen Elizabeth II adopted a personal flag for use in Canada. The design is made up of the arms of Canada with The Queen's own device — the initial 'E' — in the centre. The device is surmounted by the St. Edward's Crown within a gold chaplet of roses on a blue background.

When The Queen is in Canada, this flag is flown, day and night, at any building in which she is in residence. Generally, the flag is also flown at the saluting base when she conducts troop inspections, and on all vehicles in which she travels.

The Royal Cypher

The Royal Cypher is The Queen's monogram (Elizabeth II Regina) below a crown. It is used in the insignia of Orders, decorations and medals, and on various badges.

The Crown

When she ascended to the throne in 1952, Queen Elizabeth II adopted a heraldic representation of the crown closely resembling the St. Edward's Crown, which was used for her coronation.

The Governor General's Flag

While the coat of arms of the Governor General changes with each new Governor General, the flag remains the same: the crest of the arms of Canada on a blue field. The crest depicts a lion wearing the St. Edward's Crown, holding a red maple leaf in its front right paw, and standing on a wreath of red and white cloth. This flag was approved by Queen Elizabeth II in 1981.

THE CANADIAN CROWN

Canada has long been a monarchy — under the kings of France in the 16th, 17th and 18th centuries, under the British Crown in the 18th and 19th centuries, and as a kingdom in her own right from Confederation onward.

Although Queen Elizabeth II is Queen of the United Kingdom, it is not on this basis that Canadians offer her allegiance. She is, quite separately, sovereign of Canada by deliberate choice of Canadians (Her Majesty is also Queen of Australia, of Jamaica, of New Zealand, and of numerous other Commonwealth countries).

The most recent reaffirmation of the monarchy in Canada is found in the *Constitution Act, 1982*, which patriated our constitution from Britain. Any change to the position of The Queen or her representatives in Canada (the Governor General and the Lieutenant Governors) now requires the unanimous consent of the Senate, the House of Commons and the legislative assemblies of all the provinces.

The Sovereign Personifying the State

In our constitutional monarchy the Sovereign personifies the state and is the personal symbol of allegiance, unity and authority for all Canadians. Federal and provincial legislators, Cabinet ministers, public servants, military and police personnel, all swear allegiance to The Queen (not to a flag or constitution), as do new citizens at Canadian citizenship ceremonies. Canada's Constitution vests the executive powers of Canada in The Queen (although her representatives act on the advice of ministers responsible to the House of Commons or the legislative assemblies of the provinces). This explains why elections are called and laws are promulgated in The Queen's name.

The Queen and the Governor General

With the Balfour Report of 1926, the Governor General ceased to represent the British government and became the personal representative of the Sovereign in Canada. This was confirmed by the *Statute of Westminster* in 1931, an act of British Parliament which gave Canada and other dominions the authority to make their own laws. Powers of the King were gradually transferred to the Governor General, culminating in 1947 with the Letters Patent Constituting the Office of Governor General, which authorized the Governor General to exercise all the powers of the Sovereign in Canada, on the advice of the Canadian government. As the Sovereign's personal representative in Canada, the Governor General is accorded the honours and privileges of a Head of State.

Canada

THE CROWN IN CANADA — II

The Queen and the Lieutenant Governors

The relationship between the Sovereign and the Lieutenant Governors was not envisaged in the same way as it was with the Governor General at the time of Confederation in 1867. Rather than being considered as the Sovereign's direct representatives in the provinces, Lieutenant Governors were seen as the Governor General's representatives and agents of the federal government, which continues to be responsible for their appointment and the payment of their salary.

However, custom, evolution, convention and judicial decisions have changed the nature of the office. The Lieutenant Governors, though continuing to be federal appointees and holding some residual federal powers, are seen as the Sovereign's direct and personal representatives, embodying the Crown in the provinces. This means that Lieutenant Governors act in the name of The Queen in right of the province, just as the Governor General acts in the name of The Queen in right of Canada. Lieutenant Governors and the Provincial Crown, which they personify, symbolize the sovereignty of the provincial governments within the federation.

Flags of the Lieutenant Governors

During the 1980s, the governments of Ontario, New Brunswick, Saskatchewan, Alberta, Prince Edward Island, British Columbia, Manitoba and Newfoundland received approval from the Governor General to use a new standard to identify their Lieutenant Governors as the Sovereign's representatives at the provincial level. The new standard is a royal blue flag with the shield of the arms of the province surrounded by a circlet of 10 gold stylized maple leaves, representing the provinces of Canada. Above the shield is a St. Edward's crown, which symbolizes the dignity of the Lieutenant Governor as the Sovereign's representative in the province.

Since 1952, the Lieutenant Governor of Quebec has used a blue flag charged with the arms of Quebec within a white disk; the so-called Tudor's Crown surmounts the arms, as it was the use at the time. Nova Scotia continues to use a flag approved by Queen Victoria in 1869: it includes the Royal Union Flag (Union Jack), charged with the shield of arms of the province within a white disk circled by a garland of green maple leaves.

Ontario

Quebec

Nova Scotia

Prince Edward Island

New Brunswick

Saskatchewan

Manitoba

Alberta

British Columbia

Newfoundland

Canada

The National Anthem

"O Canada" was proclaimed Canada's national anthem on July 1, 1980, 100 years after it was first sung in Quebec City on June 24, 1880. The music was composed by Calixa Lavallée, a well-known composer, born in Verchères, Quebec in 1842. French lyrics to accompany the music were written by Adolphe-Basile Routhier, born in St-Placide, Quebec in 1839. Many English versions have appeared over the years. The version on which the official English lyrics are based was written in 1908 by Robert Stanley Weir, born in Hamilton, Ontario in 1856.

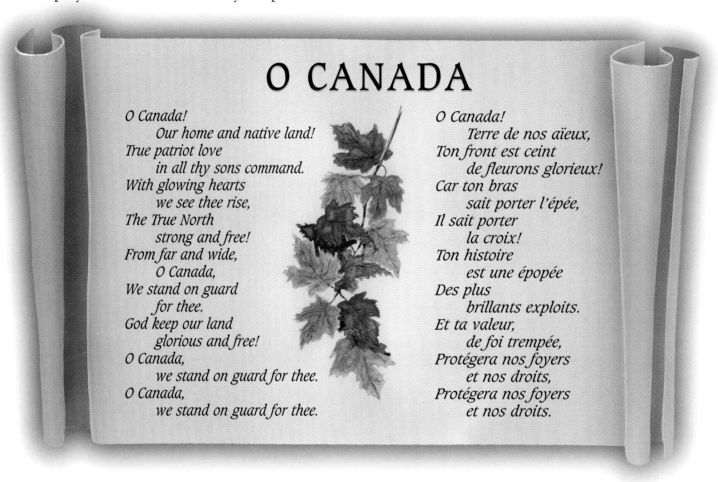

O CANADA

O Canada!
    Our home and native land!
True patriot love
    in all thy sons command.
With glowing hearts
    we see thee rise,
The True North
    strong and free!
From far and wide,
    O Canada,
We stand on guard
    for thee.
God keep our land
    glorious and free!
O Canada,
    we stand on guard for thee.
O Canada,
    we stand on guard for thee.

O Canada!
    Terre de nos aïeux,
Ton front est ceint
    de fleurons glorieux!
Car ton bras
    sait porter l'épée,
Il sait porter
    la croix!
Ton histoire
    est une épopée
Des plus
    brillants exploits.
Et ta valeur,
    de foi trempée,
Protégera nos foyers
    et nos droits,
Protégera nos foyers
    et nos droits.

OTHER CANADIAN SYMBOLS
The Maple Leaf

The maple leaf has been associated with Canada since the 1700s. In 1834, the St-Jean-Baptiste Society made the maple leaf its emblem. In 1848, the Toronto literary annual The Maple Leaf referred to it as the chosen emblem of Canada. By 1860, the maple leaf was incorporated into the badge of the 100th Regiment (Royal Canadians) and was used extensively in decorations for the visit of the Prince of Wales to Canada that year.

Alexander Muir wrote The Maple Leaf Forever as a song for Confederation in 1867; it was regarded as the national song for several decades. The coats of arms created the next year for Ontario and Quebec both included the maple leaf.

The maple leaf today appears on the penny. However, between 1876 and 1901, it appeared on all Canadian coins. The modern one-cent piece has two maple

leaves on a common twig, a design that has gone almost unchanged since 1937.

During World War I, the maple leaf was included in the badge of the Canadian Expeditionary Force. Since 1921, the arms of Canada have included three maple leaves as a distinctive Canadian emblem. Since the adoption of the national flag of Canada in 1965, the maple leaf has become Canada's most prominent symbol.

The Beaver

After the early European explorers realized that Canada was not the spice-rich Orient, the main mercantile attraction became the beaver, which numbered in the millions. Fur hats, made from beaver pelts, were the height of fashion in Europe in the late 1600s and early 1700s. As these hats became more popular, the demand for beaver pelts grew.

King Henry IV of France saw the fur trade as an opportunity to establish a North American empire and to acquire much-needed revenue. Both French and English fur traders were soon selling beaver pelts in Europe at 20 times their original purchase price.

During the peak of the fur trade, 100,000 beaver pelts were being shipped to Europe each year. The trade in pelts proved so lucrative for the Hudson's Bay Company that it honoured the buck-toothed little animal with a place on the shield of its coat of arms in 1678. The shield consists of four beavers separated by a red St. George's Cross. A coin was also created to equal the value of one beaver pelt.

Also, in 1678 Louis de Buade de Frontenac, Governor of New France, suggested the beaver as a suitable emblem for the colony, and proposed it be included in the arms of Quebec City. In 1690, in commemoration of France's successful defence of Quebec, the "Kebeca Liberata" medal was struck: a seated woman, representing France, with a beaver at her feet, representing Canada, appeared on the back of the medal.

When Montreal was incorporated as a city in 1833, the beaver was included in its coat of arms. However, it was Sir Sandford Fleming who assured the beaver a position as a national symbol when he featured it on the first Canadian postage stamp — the "Three Penny Beaver" of 1851.

Despite all this recognition, the beaver was in danger of being wiped out by the mid-19th century. Fortunately, at about that time, Europeans took a liking to silk hats and the demand for beaver pelts all but disappeared.

The beaver became an emblem of Canada's sovereignty in 1975 when it was recognized by an Act of Parliament.

Today, thanks to conservation and silk hats, the beaver — the largest rodent in Canada — is alive and well all over the country.

Official Colours

The history of the official colours of Canada goes all the way back to the first crusade in the 11th century. Bohémond I, a Norman lord, had red crosses cut from cloaks and distributed to 10,000 crusaders. The crusaders wore the crosses on their clothes as a distinguishing mark, since they had no uniform to indicate their identity.

In succeeding crusades, each nation was identified by a cross of a different colour. For a long time, France used a red cross on its banners, while England carried a white cross. In the course of history, red and white alternated as the national colours of France and England.

Red and white became Canada's official colours in the proclamation of the arms of Canada by King George V in 1921.

Tartans

There is no official tartan for Canada. However, the maple leaf tartan was approved for use in the Canadian Armed Forces in 1970, and the Court of Lord Lyon, King of Arms of Scotland, approved a tartan for the Royal Canadian Air Force in 1942.

Canada

"God Save the Queen"

The Royal Anthem originated as a patriotic song in London, England, in 1745. Neither the author nor the composer is known. The anthem is performed officially in Canada in the presence of members of the Royal Family, and as part of the Salute accorded to the Governor General and Lieutenant Governors.

GOD SAVE THE QUEEN

God save our gracious Queen!
Long live our noble Queen!
God save the Queen!
Send her victorious,
Happy and glorious,
Long to reign over us,
God save the Queen!

DIEU PROTÈGE LA REINE

Dieu protège la Reine
De sa main souveraine!
Vive la Reine!
Qu'un règne glorieux,
Long et victorieux
Rende son peuple heureux.
Vive la Reine!

Royal Union Flag

(or Union Jack)

The original Royal Union Flag was first raised in Canada at the British settlement in Newfoundland after 1610. Following the *Act of Union* between Great Britain and Ireland in 1801, the Royal Union Flag was proclaimed in its present form. In 1870, it was incorporated into the flags of the Governor General and the Lieutenant Governors of the provinces of Ontario, Quebec, Nova Scotia and New Brunswick.

The Royal Union Flag was affirmed as a Canadian symbol in 1904 and was the flag under which Canadian troops fought during the First World War. In 1964, Parliament approved the continued use of the Royal Union Flag as a symbol of Canada's membership in the Commonwealth of Nations and of her allegiance to the Crown.

Today, the Royal Union Flag is flown along with the Canadian flag at federal buildings, airports and military bases on special occasions, such as the Sovereign's birthday, the anniversary of the *Statute of Westminster* (December 11), and during Royal visits.

The Union Jack is prominent in the arms of British Columbia and in the flags of Ontario, Manitoba and British Columbia.

THE COMMONWEALTH

The Commonwealth is a loose, voluntary association of Britain and most of her former colonies, including Canada. The Commonwealth, with over fifty independent member countries, comprises about a quarter of the world's population.

Countries belong to the Commonwealth because they value it as an association. It spans all continents and forms a bridge between races and religions and between rich and poor. It enables people to discuss their common problems frankly and to work together in finding solutions.

The Commonwealth became a reality in 1931 when the independence of the dominions of Canada, Australia, New Zealand and South Africa was legally recognized in the *Statute of Westminster*. It began to take its modern form with the granting of independence to India in 1947. Two years later, India became a republic and the Commonwealth adapted itself to accept countries that owed no allegiance to the British Crown. Today, regardless of their form of government, all Commonwealth countries regard Queen Elizabeth II as a symbol of the association and, as such, Head of the Commonwealth.

The Commonwealth has grown as former colonies in Asia, Africa, the Caribbean, the Mediterranean and the Pacific were granted their independence and chose to remain members of the association.

Each Commonwealth member is free to follow its own policies, but all subscribe to a set of common ideals agreed to by Commonwealth heads of government in 1971. By adopting the Declaration of Commonwealth Principles, Commonwealth nations expressed their commitment to international peace and order, equal rights for all citizens and liberty of the individual. Member countries are also united in their opposition to colonial domination and racial oppression, and in their commitment to achieving a fairer global society.

The Commonwealth Flag

The Commonwealth Flag consists of the Commonwealth symbol in gold on a blue background. The symbol consists of a radial grating forming the letter "C" surrounding a circular solid on which are superimposed five

latitudinal lines and five longitudinal lines to represent the globe.

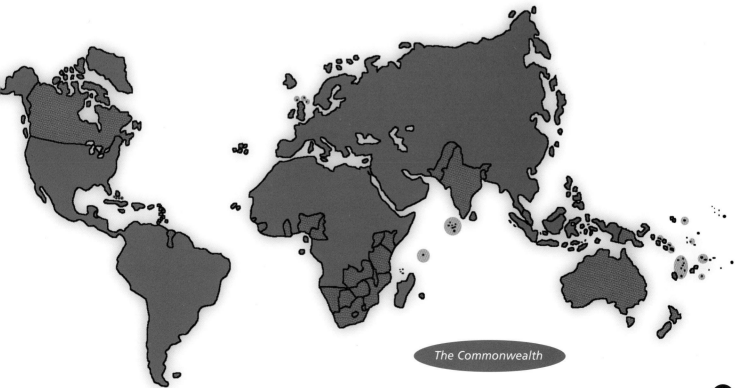

The Commonwealth

LA FRANCOPHONIE

Canada

Quebec

New Brunswick

Canada and the Canadian Francophonie

There are two official languages in Canada — French and English — with French being the mother tongue of 6.6 million Canadians (1996 census). This large Francophone community is an integral part of Canada's identity and contributes to its unique character.

The vast majority of Francophones live in Quebec, the centre of Francophone culture in North America. Almost one million Francophones live in Canada's other provinces and territories.

Since the second half of the 19th century, minority-community Francophones have come together within organizations, federations and associations that ensure the development of their communities. Over the years, the Francophone communities of Canada have adopted flags as symbols of their pride and vitality:

The Acadian national flag was adopted at the second national convention of Acadians held in Miscouche, Prince Edward Island in 1884. It is the symbol of Acadians from Nova Scotia, New Brunswick and Prince Edward Island. The flag

Acadian (1884)

mirrors the national flag of France and the star represents Our Lady of the Assumption — patron saint of Acadians.

The green and white of the Franco-Ontarian flag symbolize Ontario summers and winters. The fleur-de-lis represents affiliation with the international Francophone community, while the trillium is Ontario's official floral emblem.

Franco-Ontarian (1975)

The flag of the Fransaskois has adopted the colours of Saskatchewan. Yellow symbolizes the wheat fields, green the pine forests, and red — the colour of the heart — represents the province's Francophones. The cross is a

Fransaskois (1979)

solemn testimony to the missionaries who founded most of the Francophone settlements in Saskatchewan, while the fleur-de-lis is a symbol of the worldwide Francophone community.

The Franco-Manitoban flag is adorned with a red band representing the Red River and a yellow one representing Manitoba's wheat. The deep green roots turn into a leafy plant that is also a stylized "F" signifying Francophone.

Franco-Manitoban (1980)

The Franco-Columbian flag features the dogwood, the floral emblem of British Columbia. The blue lines evoke images of the sea, while the raised lines represent the Rocky Mountains. The fleur-

Franco-Columbian (1982)

de-lis symbolizes the Francophone community; one of the petals is pointing towards the sun, represented by the yellow circle.

The Franco-Albertan flag is blue, white and red. The fleur-de-lis symbolizes France; the stylized wild rose and the blue, Alberta; the white, the worldwide Francophone community. The blue and white bands represent the waterways and routes used by the explorers and colonists.

Franco-Albertan (1982)

The blue in the flag of the Francophone community in Yukon symbolizes the worldwide Francophone community; the gold evokes the 1898 Gold Rush; and the white symbolizes the snow that covers the Yukon landscape for a good part of the year.

Francophone community in Yukon (1985)

The blue, white and red of the flag of Newfoundland and Labrador's Francophone community represent the community's French origins. The two yellow sails, the colour of Acadia, signify the arrival of their common ancestors. The upper sail is decorated with a tamarack branch, the emblem of Labrador, and the large sail has a pitcher plant, the official floral emblem of the province.

Francophone community in Newfoundland and Labrador (1986)

The flag of the Francophone community in the Northwest Territories presents a curve with a bear. White symbolizes the snow and blue the Francophone community the world over. The curve represents the Territories' location above the 60th parallel, close to the North Pole. The polar bear, symbol of freedom and nature in the spacious North, is looking at the snowflake and the fleur-de-lis, which represents the Francophone community in the North.

Francophone community in the Northwest Territories (1992)

Canada and the international Francophonie

The term Francophonie was first used at the end of the 19th century to refer to countries under France's influence. Today, it refers to the community of peoples around the world who speak French or use it to varying degrees in their own countries or internationally.

The Francophonie also describes the network of 52 states and governments from every region of the world that share the use of the French language. At the international level, the Francophonie promotes cultural, scientific, technical and economic cooperation among its member.

Recognizing the importance of the French fact at home and abroad, the Government of Canada has associated itself with the Francophonie from its beginning in 1970. Over the past 30 years Canada has played an important role in the creation and development of the Francophonie's many institutions.

The Francophonie is a natural extension of Canada's linguistic configuration on the international scene. At the international level, it is viewed as a natural sphere of influence for Canada, comparable to its role in the Americas through the Organization of American States, in the English-speaking world through the Commonwealth, and in the Western world through the North Atlantic Treaty Organization (NATO). At the domestic level, the Francophonie is regarded as a means of highlighting Canada's linguistic duality and as a vehicle for reaffirming and developing the French fact in Canada.

Canada has the status of member state in the Francophonie, while the provinces of Quebec and New Brunswick are recognized as participating governments.

The flags of Canada, Quebec and New Brunswick officially represent the Canadian Francophonie within the international Francophonie.

The spherical form of the flag of the Francophonie conveys the idea of coming together. The five interconnected rings represent the idea of cooperation across the five continents where the members of the Francophonie are located. The five colours represent the various colours found on the flags of the participating countries and governments.

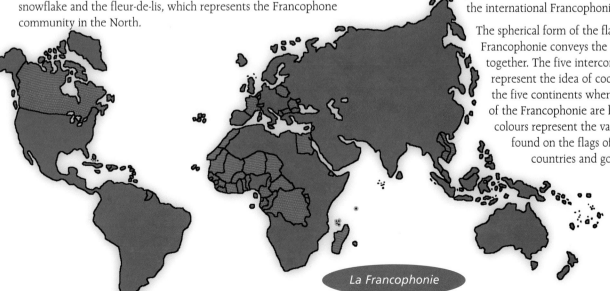

La Francophonie

Canada

HISTORICAL FLAGS

St. George's Cross

The St. George's Cross, which is prominent in many provincial and territorial coats of arms, traces its history back to the legend of St. George, the patron saint of England at the time of the Crusades. The red cross associated with St. George came into wide use as a national emblem of England in 1274, during the reign of Edward I. The earliest recorded use of the St. George's Cross in Canada is found in a water colour painting that depicts English explorers skirmishing with Inuit, almost certainly on Baffin Island during Martin Frobisher's expedition of 1577. The St. George's Cross was later incorporated into the coats of arms of the Hudson's Bay Company and the Canada Company, a land settlement and colonization company operating in Upper Canada in the first half of the 19th century.

Fleur-de-lis

The fleur-de-lis was a symbol of French sovereignty in Canada from 1534, when Jacques Cartier landed at Gaspé and claimed the newly explored territory in the name of Francis I of France, until the early 1760s, when Canada was ceded to the United Kingdom. The Royal Arms of France, with its three gold fleurs-de-lis on a blue field, was the royal emblem displayed whenever French explorers claimed new land in North America.

The "bannière de France" or Banner of France, which also displayed three gold fleurs-de-lis on a blue field, was raised by fur trader Pierre de Monts at the settlement on Île Sainte-Croix in 1604, and a swallow-tailed flag with fleurs-de-lis flew from Champlain's Habitation at Quebec in 1608. With the death of King Henry IV in 1610, the "bannière" ceased to be used as a national flag.

During the first half of the 17th century, the inhabitants of New France viewed the white flag of the "marine royale" as the flag of the French nation. This same flag was widely used after New France became a royal province by an edict of Louis XIV in 1663.

The fleur-de-lis reappeared as a symbol of French heritage in the arms granted to Quebec by Queen Victoria in 1868. In 1948, the Quebec government adopted the "fleurdelisé" as its provincial flag. The fleur-de-lis also appears in the coats of arms of Canada and New Brunswick.

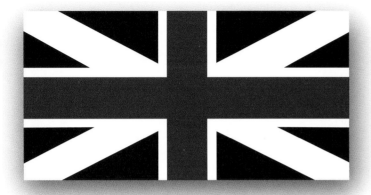

Royal Union Flag (1606 - 1800)

Following the Treaty of Paris in 1763, the official British flag was the two-crossed jack or the Royal Union Flag. First proclaimed as a royal flag in 1606 after James VI of Scotland became James I of England, it combined England's flag of a red St. George's Cross on a white background with Scotland's flag, a white St. Andrew's Cross on a dark blue background. After the legislative union of England and Scotland in 1708, the Union Flag was adopted as the Royal Flag for the two united kingdoms.

In the years between the Treaty of Paris and the American Revolution, the Royal Union Flag was supposed to be used at all British establishments on the North American continent, from Newfoundland to the Gulf of Mexico. In practice, however, it was frequently replaced by the Red Ensign, the flag of the British merchant marine, which featured a Royal Union Flag on a red background.

After the American Revolution, those colonists who remained loyal to the Crown and fought under the Red Ensign settled in many parts of what are now Ontario, New Brunswick and Nova Scotia. The Red Ensign is often referred to as the flag of Canada's United Empire Loyalists.

Following the *Act of Union* between Great Britain and Ireland in 1801, the diagonal Cross of St. Patrick, red on white, was incorporated into the Royal Union Flag, giving it its present-day configuration.

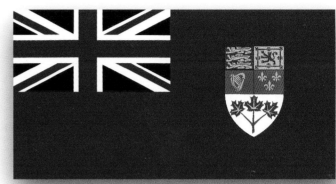

Canadian Red Ensign

From about 1870 to 1904, the Red Ensign was used on land and sea as Canada's flag, with the quartered arms of the provinces in the fly frequently surrounded by branches of maple leaves and oak, surmounted by the Royal Crown and displaying a beaver on a log below. In 1892, the British Admiralty approved the use of the Red Ensign for Canadian use at sea. This gave rise to the name 'the Canadian Red Ensign'.

By the beginning of the 20th century, the shield of the Canadian Red Ensign featured the arms of the seven provinces then in Confederation. In 1924, the Canadian government replaced this unofficial shield with the shield of the Arms of Canada in the fly of the flag. This new version of the flag was approved for use on Canadian government buildings abroad. In Canada, the Canadian Red Ensign flew over federal buildings from 1945 until 1965, when it was replaced by the red and white maple leaf flag.

Canada

HISTORICAL BOUNDARIES

Map 1
1867

1867 - The new Dominion of Canada is no larger than Nova Scotia, New Brunswick, the land near the Gulf of St. Lawrence, the St. Lawrence River and the north side of the Great Lakes.

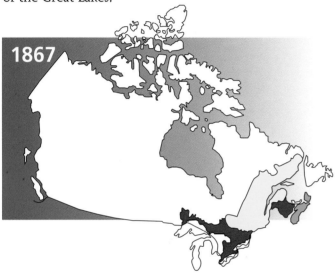

Map 2
1870 to 1873

1870 - The British government transfers control of the North-Western Territory to Canada. The Hudson's Bay Company sells Rupert's Land to the new nation. The province of Manitoba is created out of this vast area. The new province, made up of land around the Red River, is small by Canadian standards — 36,000 square kilometres. The rest of the newly-acquired land is called the Northwest Territories.

1871 - The colony of British Columbia becomes a province of Canada.

1873 - The small island colony of Prince Edward Island, which had rejected Confederation six years earlier, joins the union.

Map 3
1874 to 1882

1874 - Boundaries for the province of Ontario are established.

1876 - The District of Keewatin, in the Northwest Territories, is created.

1880 - The British transfer ownership of the islands of the Arctic archipelago to Canada.

1881 - Manitoba's boundaries are extended for the first time. The new area added to Manitoba was part of the area given to Ontario in 1874. This causes conflict between Manitoba and her neighbouring province.

1882 - The Districts of Assiniboia, Saskatchewan, Alberta and Athabaska are formed in the Northwest Territories.

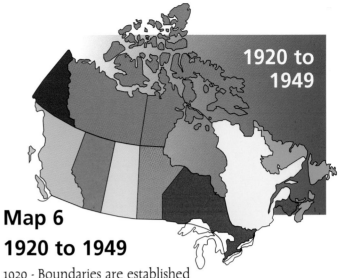

Map 4
1884 to 1905

1889 - The boundary dispute between Manitoba and Ontario is settled in Ontario's favour.

1895 - The Districts of Ungava, Franklin, Mackenzie and Yukon are created in the Northwest Territories.

1898 - Quebec's boundaries are extended

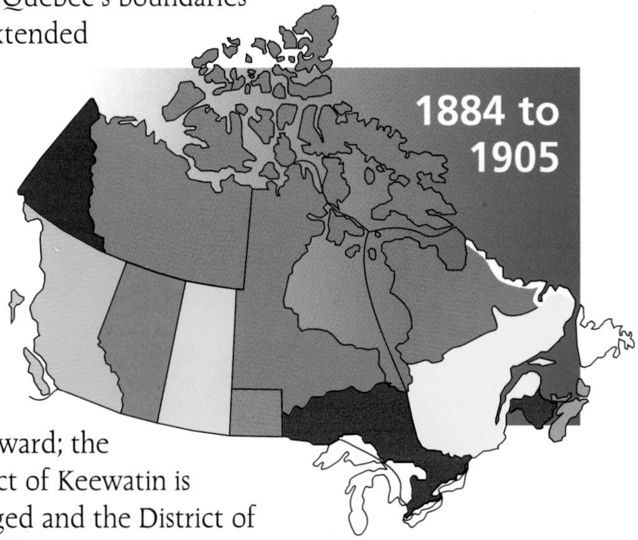

northward; the District of Keewatin is enlarged and the District of Yukon becomes a separate territory.

1903 - The British Columbia-Alaska boundary dispute is settled.

1905 - The provinces of Alberta and Saskatchewan are created out of the Districts of Athabaska, Alberta, Saskatchewan and Assiniboia; the District of Keewatin is transferred to the newly-defined Northwest Territories.

Map 6
1920 to 1949

1920 - Boundaries are established among the districts of the Northwest Territories.

1927 - The Quebec-Labrador boundary is delineated by Judicial Committee of the British Privy Council.

1949 - Newfoundland and Labrador join Confederation, becoming Canada's tenth province.

Map 7
1999

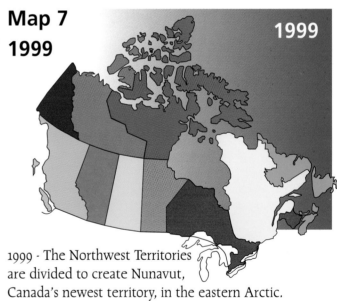

1999 - The Northwest Territories are divided to create Nunavut, Canada's newest territory, in the eastern Arctic.

Map 5
1912

1912 - The boundaries of Quebec, Ontario and Manitoba are extended northward to Hudson Bay and Hudson Strait.

ONTARIO

Origin of the Name

The word Ontario comes from the Iroquois word "kanadario," meaning "sparkling water." The province is aptly named: lakes and rivers make up one fifth of its area. In 1641, "Ontario" described the land along the north shore of the easternmost part of the Great Lakes. Later, the southern part of the province was referred to as "Old Ontario." The name "Ontario" was adapted for the new era that began in 1867, when the area became a province.

Population (1999) 11,548,000
Area: Land . . . . . .891,190 km²
        Fresh Water . .177,390 km²
        Total . . . . .1,068,580 km²
Capital: . . . . .Toronto
Date of entry into Confederation:
July 1, 1867

TORONTO

History

Ontario was first inhabited by the Algonquian and Iroquoian-speaking tribes. The most important Algonquian tribe in Ontario was the Ojibwa, which lived in northern Ontario. There were two major Iroquoian confederacies: the Iroquois and the Huron. The Five Nations of the Iroquois (Seneca, Oneida, Onondaga, Cayuga and Mohawk) lived near Lake Ontario and Lake Erie. The five Huron tribes inhabited the area near Lake Simcoe.

These tribes were highly developed politically and culturally by the time the Europeans penetrated the area. In 1610, Henry Hudson became the first European to set foot in Ontario. Samuel de Champlain and Étienne Brûlé first established contact with the Indians of southern Ontario in 1613.

By 1774, the British controlled what is now southern Ontario, then part of the Province of Quebec. The *Constitutional Act* of 1791, which split the province in two, renamed

White Pine

the area Upper Canada. Although French-Canadians were and remain a significant proportion of Ontario's population, the great influx of Loyalists after the American Revolution helped force the separation.

Accustomed to autonomy in the American colonies, the Loyalists demanded changes in their new homeland. Rebellions against undemocratic government in 1837, in both Upper and Lower Canada, prompted the British to send Lord Durham to report on the troubles.

As a result of Durham's recommendations, the *Act of Union* of 1840 joined Upper and Lower Canada once again, this time as the Province of Canada. Although a more democratic and responsible government resulted, the union was not a success: Canada East and Canada West continued to be two distinct regions. They entered the confederation conferences of 1864 as though they were separate, and became different provinces — Ontario and Quebec — at Confederation in 1867.

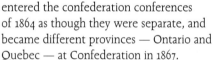

Coat of Arms

Ontario is Canada's second largest and most populous province. At Confederation, the province was little larger than present-day southern Ontario. Bitter border disputes with Manitoba over the area north of Lake Superior ended in 1889, when the area became part of Ontario. The rest of Northern Ontario was annexed in 1912 when Ontario expanded to its current size.

Coat of Arms

Ontario was granted its coat of arms by Queen Victoria in 1868. The arms were augmented with a crest, supporters and motto by King Edward VII in 1909.

The red Cross of St. George, symbolic of England, appears in the upper third of the shield. The lower portion of the shield features three golden maple leaves, emblematic of Canada, on a green background.

The shield is supported by a moose and a Canadian deer; a black bear appears on the crest above the shield.

Ontario is the only province or territory that has a stylized coat of arms. This means that the arms are not open to individual interpretation by artists.

Motto

UT INCEPIT FIDELIS SIC PERMANET
(Loyal she began and loyal she remains)

Flag

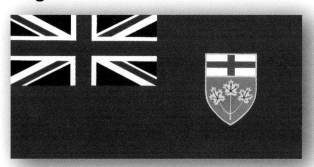

The Flag of Ontario was adopted by the Legislature in 1965, with Queen Elizabeth II approving the use of the Royal Union Flag (Union Jack) within the flag design the same year.

Ontario's flag closely resembles the Canadian Red Ensign. The Union Jack occupies the upper quarter near the staff, while the shield of arms of Ontario is centred in the fly half of the flag. The proportions of the flag are two by length and one by width.

Floral Emblem

Ontario's floral emblem, the white trillium, was adopted in 1937. It blooms in late April and May. The blooms are very sensitive to light, and the white flowers usually bend toward the sun as it moves across the sky. The white trillium is found in the deciduous forests and woodlands of Ontario.

The adoption of an official flower for Ontario grew out of a movement during the First World War to choose a national floral emblem appropriate for planting on the graves of Canadian servicemen overseas. The trillium was proposed by the Ottawa Horticultural Society. Although it was well received, no national flower was ever chosen.

Other Provincial Symbols

Tree: White Pine

Bird: Common Loon

Gemstone: Amethyst

Colours: Green and Yellow

Common Loon

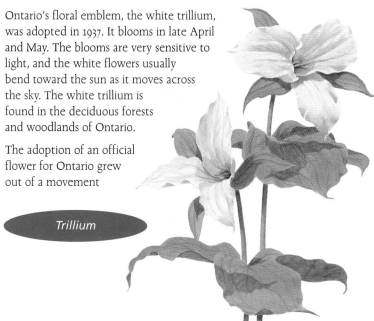

Trillium

Amethyst

QUEBEC

Origin of the Name

The name Quebec comes from the Algonquin word for "narrow passage" or "strait" and was first used to describe the narrowing of the St. Lawrence River near Quebec City. Quebec has had several names throughout its history: Canada, New France, Lower Canada and Canada East.

History

The original inhabitants of Quebec were Indian tribes, mostly of the Algonquian and Iroquoian linguistic groups, who greatly influenced the early history of the province. Among the Algonquian tribes were the Naskapi-Montagnais and the Algonquin. The Iroquoian included the Seneca, Oneida, Onondaga, Cayuga and the Mohawk. Northern Quebec was, and largely is, inhabited by Inuit.

Quebec was one of the first areas of Canada to be explored and settled by Europeans. Jacques Cartier landed at Gaspé in 1534 and claimed the land in the name of King Francis I of France.

After the Treaty of Paris in 1763, New France was ceded to the British. An area including what is now southern Quebec and parts of present-day Ontario was renamed the Province of Quebec by the British.

In 1791, the province was divided into Upper and Lower Canada to accommodate the sudden influx of Loyalists from the American colonies to the western half of the province (present-day Ontario). After rebellions in both Upper and Lower Canada in 1837, the two were reunited by the *Act of Union* in 1840, becoming the Province of Canada.

However, the union was not successful. Canada East and Canada West, as they came to be known, retained their separate identities. Nevertheless, they knew that some kind of alliance was the best way of achieving greater independence from both Britain and the United States. When the province entered into Confederation with Nova Scotia and New Brunswick in 1867, Canada East became the new Province of Quebec, and Canada West became the Province of Ontario.

The area of Quebec was increased first in 1898 and again in 1912, when its boundaries were redefined to include the District of Ungava, formerly part of the Northwest Territories. A boundary dispute between Canada and Newfoundland over the exact border between Labrador and Quebec was decided by the Judicial Committee of the British Privy Council in 1927.

Quebec is the largest province in Canada. It is three times the size of France and seven times larger than Great Britain.

Coat of Arms

Coat of Arms

The Quebec coat of arms was granted by Queen Victoria in 1868, and revised by Order of the Lieutenant Governor in Council in 1939.

The shield features three gold fleurs-de-lis on a blue field, a reminder of Royal France which once ruled Quebec. (The original

Population (1999)	7,355,000
Area: Land	......1,356,790 km²
Fresh Water	..183,890 km²
Total	.....1,540,680 km²
Capital	...........Quebec City
Date of entry into Confederation:	July 1, 1867

QUEBEC CITY

Yellow Birch

coat of arms, granted by Queen Victoria, had two blue fleurs-de-lis on a gold background.) A sprig of three green maple leaves, representative of the Quebec's numerous maple trees, is displayed in the lower portion. The gold lion in the shield's centre represents the British Crown that granted the shield.

nation. The madonna lily is native to southeastern Europe and Asia Minor but can be cultivated in most parts of Eastern Canada and British Columbia. It is one of the most fragrant and beautiful members of the lily family.

Motto

JE ME SOUVIENS
(I remember)

Other Provincial Symbols

Tree: Yellow Birch

Bird: Snowy Owl

Snowy Owl

Flag

The Quebec flag was adopted by Order of the Lieutenant Governor in Council in 1948 and confirmed by the province's legislature in 1950.

Quebec's flag is generally known as the "fleurdelisé". The white cross on a blue field recalls an ancient French military banner, and the four fleurs-de-lis are symbolic of France. The flag's proportions are three by length and two by width

Floral Emblem

Quebec's floral emblem, the white garden lily, was adopted in 1963. The white garden lily (or madonna lily) is the only official provincial or territorial flower that does not grow naturally in Canada. It was chosen as Quebec's emblem because of its resemblance to the fleur-de-lis, symbolic of France, the province's founding

White Garden Lily

NOVA SCOTIA

Origin of the Name

Nova Scotia was named by Sir William Alexander, who received a grant to all the land between New England and Newfoundland from King James VI of Scotland (King James I of England) in 1621. The official charter was in Latin and the name "New Scotland" retained its Latin form — Nova Scotia.

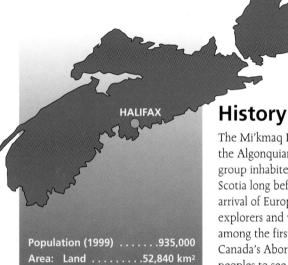

HALIFAX

Population (1999) 935,000
Area: Land . . . . .52,840 km²
        Fresh Water . . . .2,650 km²
        Total . . . . .55,490 km²
Capital . . . . .Halifax
Date of entry into Confederation:
July 1, 1867

History

The Mi'kmaq Indians of the Algonquian linguistic group inhabited Nova Scotia long before the arrival of European explorers and were among the first of Canada's Aboriginal peoples to see Europeans. The Mi'kmaq allied themselves with the French throughout early Canadian history, helping them adjust to the land and fight against the British.

All of Nova Scotia, as well as parts of Quebec, New Brunswick and Maine, was originally known as Acadia and mainly settled by the French. Fur trader Pierre de Monts established the first successful agricultural settlement in Canada at Port-Royal (now Annapolis Royal, Nova Scotia) in 1605. For the next century, the British and the French fought over the area. Control passed back and forth until 1713, when all of Acadia, except Île Royale (now Cape Breton Island), was ceded to the British under the Treaty of Utrecht.

Red Spruce

After the Seven Years War, Nova Scotia included Saint John's Island (as Prince Edward Island was then known), Cape Breton Island and the area now known as New Brunswick. In 1769, Saint John's Island separated from Nova Scotia. In 1784, after a great influx of loyalist refugees from the United States, Nova Scotia was partitioned to create the colonies of New Brunswick and Cape Breton Island. However, Cape Breton again became part of Nova Scotia in 1820.

Coat of Arms

Nova Scotia's coat of arms, granted in 1625, is by far the oldest of any province or territory. The shield features the Cross of St. Andrew. To differentiate between Scotland and Nova Scotia, the colours of the cross are reversed: blue on white. At the centre of the Nova Scotia shield is the shield of the Royal Arms of Scotland, containing a royal lion within a double red border on a field of yellow or gold.

Coat of Arms

The crest above the shield features two hands, one armed and the other bare, supporting a laurel and a thistle. One interpretation of this has the armed hand and the thistle representing the vow of the King of the Scots to protect his subjects, and the bare hand and the laurel sprig representing the conquest of hardships to be met in Nova Scotia. The laurel sprig is a symbol of peace, triumph and conquest.

The shield is supported by a crowned unicorn, part of Scotland's royal coat of arms, and an Aboriginal man, representing the province's native Indian population.

A royal helmet — facing forward — rests on the shield. A unique feature of the Nova Scotia coat of arms is that the motto is placed above the arms, a common practice in Scotland.

Nova Scotia is the only province to have had a coat of arms annulled. When the province joined Confederation, it was awarded a new coat of arms, as were the other new provinces. Unlike the other provinces, however, Nova Scotia had already been granted one. After the First World War, there was a movement to restore the province's original arms. This change received royal approval in 1929.

Motto

MUNIT HAEC ET ALTERA VINCIT
(One defends and the other conquers)

Flag

The flag of Nova Scotia was the first flag in the overseas Commonwealth to be authorized by royal charter. It is derived from the ancient arms granted in 1625 by King Charles I. The flag features the province's shield extended in a rectangular shape. The flag's proportions are four by length and three by width.

Osprey

Floral Emblem

Nova Scotia's floral emblem, the mayflower, was adopted in 1901.

The mayflower, also known as trailing arbutus, blooms in the forest glades of early spring, often amid the last remaining snows of winter. The pink flowers are delicately scented and grow on stems from 15 to 30 centimetres long. The mayflower derives its name from the Massachusetts pilgrims who saw it as the first flower of spring and named it after the ship that brought them to Plymouth Rock.

Other Provincial Symbols

Tartan: The Nova Scotia Tartan (the first provincial-territorial tartan in Canada; registered with the Court of the Lord Lyon, King of Arms of Scotland in 1956).

Tree: Red Spruce

Bird: Osprey

Dog: Nova Scotia Duck Tolling Retriever

Berry: Wild Blueberry

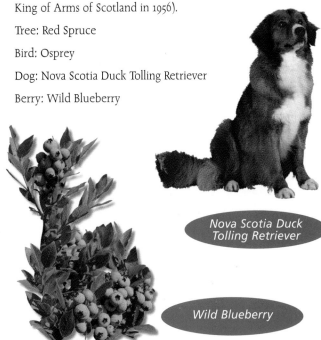

Nova Scotia Duck Tolling Retriever

Mayflower

Wild Blueberry

NEW BRUNSWICK

Origin of the Name

New Brunswick was named in 1784 to honour the reigning British monarch, King George III, who was also Duke of Brunswick and a member of the House of Hanover.

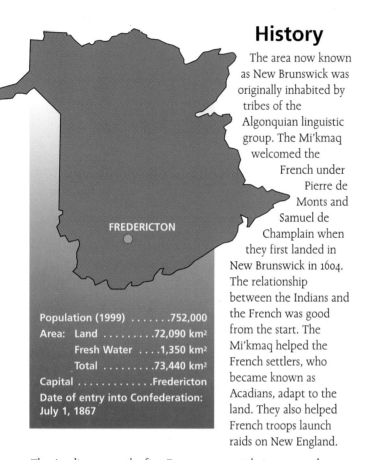

FREDERICTON

Population (1999) 752,000	
Area: Land . . . . .72,090 km²	
Fresh Water . . . .1,350 km²	
Total . . . . .73,440 km²	
Capital . . . . .Fredericton	
Date of entry into Confederation: July 1, 1867	

History

The area now known as New Brunswick was originally inhabited by tribes of the Algonquian linguistic group. The Mi'kmaq welcomed the French under Pierre de Monts and Samuel de Champlain when they first landed in New Brunswick in 1604. The relationship between the Indians and the French was good from the start. The Mi'kmaq helped the French settlers, who became known as Acadians, adapt to the land. They also helped French troops launch raids on New England.

The Acadians were the first Europeans to settle in present-day New Brunswick. Until the Treaty of Utrecht in 1713, when France ceded the area to Great Britain, both Nova Scotia and New Brunswick were part of Acadia. However, over the years, France had all but ignored the Acadians, being much more concerned with New France and the increasing value of the fur trade there.

The Treaty of Utrecht created the British colony of Nova Scotia, which at that time included New Brunswick and Prince Edward Island. Nevertheless, Acadia continued for many years to be an area of conflict between the old world powers, falling eventually to Britain. After the British victory, many Acadians fled; others were expelled by the authorities in 1755.

In 1762, a trading community was established at the mouth of the St. John River by Massachusetts merchants. Before the peace of 1763, permanent British settlements were started by New Englanders at Chignecto and in the St. John River Valley. Settlers from Yorkshire, England, who came to Chignecto in the early 1770s, helped defeat an attempt from the rebellious colonies in 1776 to take Chignecto, and its strategic Fort Cumberland/Beauséjour.

In 1783, thousands of Loyalist refugees from the American Revolution settled in the western part of Nova Scotia, far from the colony's administrative centre in Halifax. In response to Loyalist demands for their own colonial administration, the British government established the new colony of New Brunswick in 1784.

SPEM REDUXIT

Coat of Arms

In 1864, New Brunswick was involved in discussions with the colonies of Nova Scotia, Prince Edward Island and Newfoundland to consider a Maritime union when the Province of Canada issued an invitation to attend the conference in Charlottetown. The result, three years later, was the creation of the Dominion of Canada.

New Brunswick was among the first four provinces to form the Dominion of Canada at Confederation on July 1, 1867. Promises of increased prosperity, a railway linking New Brunswick to central Canada, and a desire to unite with other British colonies to form a strong country in the face of growing American influence, all encouraged New Brunswick to join Confederation.

Balsam Fir

Picture Province Fly

Coat of Arms

The shield of New Brunswick's coat of arms was granted by Queen Victoria in 1868. The crest and supporters were granted and the motto confirmed by Queen Elizabeth II in 1984 to honour the 200th anniversary of New Brunswick's creation.

The upper third of the shield is red with a gold lion, symbolizing New Brunswick's ties to Britain. The lion is also found in the arms of the Duchy of Brunswick in Germany, the ancestral home of King George III. The lower part of the shield displays an ancient galley, most probably a reflection of the importance of shipbuilding and seafaring to New Brunswick in the 19th century. The galley is also based on the design of the province's original great seal, which featured a sailing ship on water.

The shield is supported by two white-tailed deer wearing collars of Indian wampum. From one collar is suspended the Royal Union Flag (the Union Jack), from the other the fleurs-de-lis to indicate the province's British and French background. Today, New Brunswick is Canada's only officially bilingual province.

The crest above the shield features an Atlantic salmon leaping from a coronet of gold maple leaves and bearing St. Edward's Crown on its back. The coat of arms base is a grassy mound with fiddleheads and purple violets, the provincial floral emblem.

Motto

SPEM REDUXIT
(Hope restored)

Flag

The New Brunswick flag was proclaimed by the province's Lieutenant Governor in 1965. Its design is based on the provincial shield of arms approved by Queen Victoria in 1868. The flag's proportions are four by length and two and one-half by width.

Floral Emblem

New Brunswick's floral emblem, the purple violet, was adopted in 1936. The flower, a relative of the pansy, can be purple or dark blue and is also known as the marsh blue violet. Its stems are from 8 to 15 centimetres long. The purple violet is found throughout Eastern Canada, particularly in wet meadows and woodlands. It grows especially well in New Brunswick and is seen in fields, lawns and gardens in the early summer.

Purple Violet

Other Provincial Symbols

Tartan: New Brunswick Tartan

Tree: Balsam Fir

Bird: Black-capped Chickadee

Fishing Fly: "Picture Province" Atlantic Salmon Fly

Black-capped Chickadee

MANITOBA

Origin of the Name

The name Manitoba likely comes from the Cree "Man-into-wah-paow," which means "the narrows of the Great Spirit." The words describe Lake Manitoba, which narrows to half a mile at its centre. The waves on the loose surface rocks of its north shore produce curious, bell-like wailing sounds, which the first Indian visitors believed came from a huge drum beaten by the spirit Manitou. The name Manitoba was given to the province at its creation in 1870 at the suggestion of Métis leader Louis Riel.

WINNIPEG

Population (1999)	1,140,000
Area: Land	.......548,360 km²
Fresh Water	..101,590 km²
Total	.......649,950 km²
Capital	.............Winnipeg

Date of entry into Confederation:
July 15, 1870

History

The Assiniboine Indians were the first inhabitants of Manitoba. Other tribes included the nomadic Cree, who followed the herds of buffalo and caribou on their seasonal migrations.

In their search for the spice-rich Orient through the Northwest Passage, Europeans reached Manitoba through Hudson Bay in the early 17th century. Unlike most of the rest of Canada, the northern parts of the province were settled before the south. In 1612, British captain Thomas Button wintered two ships at Port Nelson on Hudson Bay, near the mouths of the Nelson and Hayes Rivers. In 1690 and 1691, Henry Kelsey of the Hudson's Bay Company explored northern Manitoba from Hudson Bay as far as the Saskatchewan River, near The Pas. A party led by French fur-trader and explorer La Vérendrye traveled the Red and Winnipeg Rivers from 1733 to 1738, building several outposts.

White Spruce

In 1670, King Charles II of England granted the Hudson's Bay Company a large tract of land named Rupert's Land. The company set up fur-trading posts to exploit the country's wealth. Among their major posts were York Factory at the mouths of the Nelson and Hayes Rivers, and Prince of Wales's Fort at the mouth of the Churchill River. The latter was a large stone fort, built between 1731 and 1771. It was captured and badly damaged by the French in 1782. The Hudson's Bay Company then built Fort Churchill in 1783 and continued to use the site until 1933.

After 1740, in the wake of La Vérendrye, traders from New France pushed across the southern part of Manitoba. They were succeeded by teams of English-speaking "pedlars" and French-Canadian voyageurs who paddled swift canoes from Montreal to the West and back, seeking furs.

Intense rivalry for furs developed between the Montreal-based North West Company and the Hudson's Bay Company. Their battle for the fur trade resulted in both companies building forts throughout the plains. Alexander Mackenzie, an employee of the North West Company, pushed the chain of forts west into the Rocky Mountains and north to the Arctic. The rivalry came to its height in the Red River and Assiniboine River Valleys in Manitoba, where open warfare broke out.

Great Grey Owl

During the same period, the first European agricultural settlement was established by Lord Selkirk, a Scottish nobleman, who sent a number of dispossessed Scottish Highlanders to settle land he had secured from the Hudson's Bay Company in 1811. He called the area Assiniboia.

It was not long before the Selkirk colony was caught in the fur-trade war. In 1816, Governor Robert Semple and 19 colonists were killed at Seven Oaks in a battle with the Métis, who had been urged on by the North West Company. The settlement survived; however the violence and lengthy legal battles brought about Selkirk's impoverishment and the bankruptcy of the North West Company.

In the 1860s, the Province of Canada, anxious to expand into the great northwest, asked Britain to buy out the Hudson's Bay Company, as it had the East India Company. Although willing to request the surrender of the land from the Hudson's Bay Company, Britain insisted that the money come from Canada. Canada offered the company 300,000 pounds sterling. The company settled for the money, plus one twentieth of all the fertile land in the west and the land that surrounded their trading posts.

The inhabitants of the area were not consulted on this transaction. This, and the constant threat of an American invasion from the south, made them nervous. No clear terms were spelled out for the people of the Red River area and, during negotiations on their status, resistance developed in the colony. The Métis, a mostly French-speaking people of mixed European and Indian blood, rallied under the leadership of Louis Riel to oppose the Canadian proposals. Riel succeeded in uniting both the French and English-speaking groups to establish a locally-elected, provisional government in 1869.

Negotiations between the provisional government and the government of Canada led to Parliament passing the *Manitoba Act* of 1870, under which Manitoba joined the other provinces in Confederation.

The new province consisted of 36,000 square kilometres surrounding the Red River Valley. It was called the "postage stamp" province because of its square shape and relatively small size. However, the province did not remain that small. Its boundaries were enlarged in 1881 and again in 1912. Today, Manitoba is 650,000 square kilometres and could have been larger had it not been for an 1884 decision in favour of Ontario, which established the present-day boundary between the two provinces.

Agricultural settlement helped the province prosper in its infancy. With the help of the railway and certain acts of Parliament in the late 1800s, the province was soon filled with settlers from Eastern Canada and Europe.

Coat of Arms

Manitoba's shield was granted under King Edward VII in 1905, while its augmented coat of arms was granted by Governor General Ramon Hnatyshyn in 1992.

At the centre of the arms is the original shield featuring the Cross of St. George and a buffalo standing on a rock. Above the shield is a gold helmet signaling Manitoba's co-sovereign status in Confederation. Surmounting all is a beaver, a national symbol of Canada, holding the province's floral emblem (prairie crocus) and carrying a royal crown on its back.

The shield supporters are a unicorn, reflecting the province's early Scottish settlers, and a white horse, an animal vital to the First Peoples, the Métis and European settlers. The unicorn and the horse stand atop waters, grain fields and forests. The seven provincial flowers at the centre represent one people of diverse origins.

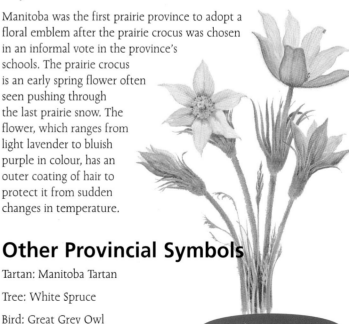

Coat of Arms

Motto

GLORIOSUS ET LIBER
(Glorious and free)

Flag

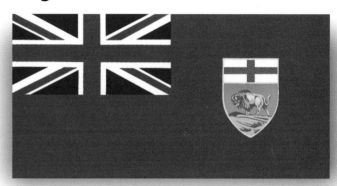

The Manitoba flag was adopted in 1966 under Queen Elizabeth II. The flag closely resembles the Canadian Red Ensign. The Union Jack occupies the upper quarter on the staff side, while the provincial shield is centred on the fly half of the flag. The flag's proportions are two by length and one by width.

Floral Emblem

The prairie crocus was adopted as Manitoba's floral emblem in 1906.

Manitoba was the first prairie province to adopt a floral emblem after the prairie crocus was chosen in an informal vote in the province's schools. The prairie crocus is an early spring flower often seen pushing through the last prairie snow. The flower, which ranges from light lavender to bluish purple in colour, has an outer coating of hair to protect it from sudden changes in temperature.

Other Provincial Symbols

Tartan: Manitoba Tartan

Tree: White Spruce

Bird: Great Grey Owl

Prairie Crocus

BRITISH COLUMBIA

Origin of the Name

The southern part of the area now known as British Columbia was called Columbia, after the Columbia River, and the central region was given the name of New Caledonia by explorer Simon Fraser. To avoid confusion with Colombia in South America and the island of New Caledonia in the Pacific ocean, Queen Victoria named the area British Columbia when it became a colony in 1858.

VICTORIA

Population(1999) 4,056,000
Area: Land . . . . . . .929,730 km²
        Fresh Water . . .18,070 km²
        Total . . . . . .947,800 km²
Capital . . . . .Victoria
Date of entry into Confederation:
July 20, 1871

History

British Columbia was inhabited by the greatest number of distinct Indian tribes of any province or territory in Canada. Because of the diversity of the Pacific coast — mild to cold climates, seashore to mountain tops — the tribes that settled in this area developed completely different cultures and languages. They were not only different from each other, but also from the rest of the Indian tribes in Canada. Among the tribes along the coastline were the Nootka, Bella Coola, Tlinkit, Haida, Tsimshian, Kwakiutl and Salish. The tribes found on the plateaus of the Rocky Mountains included the Tagish, Tahltan, Tsetsaut, Carrier, Chilcotin Interior Salish, Nicola and Kootenay.

Unlike Eastern Canada, where the French and English disputed control of the land, the first two countries to contest areas of British Columbia were Spain and Russia. In the 1700s, the Spanish claimed ownership of the west coast of North America from Mexico to Vancouver Island. At the same time, the Russians were making an overlapping claim: control of the Pacific coast from Alaska to San Francisco.

In 1778, Captain James Cook of Great Britain became the first person to actually chart the land. George Vancouver, a 20-year-old midshipman on Cook's voyage, later led three expeditions of his own and charted more than 16,000 kilometres of coastline. Having firmly established her right to the area, Britain proceeded to settle disputes with both Spain and Russia.

The 1846 Oregon Treaty with the United States gave Britain sole ownership of Vancouver Island and the area north of the 49th parallel. In 1849, Vancouver Island was granted to the Hudson's Bay Company in the hope that it might be settled. Until that time, the only European settlements in that part of the country were fur-trading posts.

Coat of Arms

When gold was discovered in the lower Fraser Valley in 1857, thousands of people came in search of instant wealth. To help maintain law and order, the British government established the separate colony of British Columbia the following year. In 1866, when the frenzy of the gold rush was over, the colony of Vancouver Island joined the colony of British Columbia.

British Columbia was separated from the rest of British North America by thousands of kilometres and the imposing Rocky Mountains. The promise of a rail link from the Pacific coast to the rest of Canada convinced the colony to join Confederation in 1871.

Western Red Cedar

Coat of Arms

The shield of British Columbia's coat of arms was granted by King Edward VII in 1906. The complete coat of arms was granted by Queen Elizabeth II in 1987.

The Union Jack, with an antique golden crown in the centre, occupies the upper third of the shield, symbolizing the Province's origin as a British colony. The bottom of the shield features a golden half-sun, superimposed upon three wavy blue bars cast horizontally on white. The blue bars represent the Pacific Ocean and the sun signifies British Columbia's location as the most westerly province in Canada.

The shield, which was designed by Victoria clergyman Arthur John Beanlands, is supported by a Wapiti Stag and a Bighorn Sheep Ram, representing the colonies of Vancouver Island and British Columbia.

The crest above the shield features a lion standing on a crown. The lion wears a garland of pacific dogwoods, the provincial flower, around its neck to differentiate it from the crest of Canada. Between the crest and shield is the golden helmet of sovereignty, a mark of British Columbia's co-sovereign status in Confederation. Above the helmet are the traditional heraldic elements of a wreath and mantling in red and white, the colours of Canada. The provincial flower is featured a second time by entwining dogwoods around the motto scroll at the base of the arms.

Motto

SPLENDOR SINE OCCASU
(Splendour without diminishment)

Flag

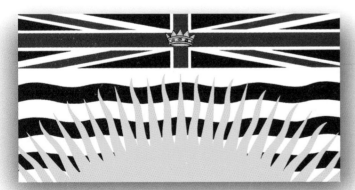

King Edward VII assigned the provincial arms and banner in 1906. The British Columbia flag, which duplicates the design of the provincial shield, was adopted by Order of the Lieutenant Governor in Council in 1960. The flag's proportions are five by length and three by width.

Floral Emblem

British Columbia's floral emblem, the pacific dogwood, was adopted in 1956. The pacific dogwood is a tree that grows from 6 to 18 metres high and flowers profusely in April and May with large white blossoms. The tree is also conspicuous in autumn with its clusters of bright red berries and brilliant foliage.

Pacific Dogwood

Other Provincial Symbols

Tartan: British Columbia Tartan

Tree: Western Red Cedar

Bird: Steller's Jay

Gemstone: Jade

Steller's Jay

Jade

Origin of the Name

The province's name was adopted in 1799 to honour Prince Edward, Duke of Kent, fourth son of King George III, who was then commander-in-chief of British North America and was stationed in Halifax when the Island was named. The prince was Queen Victoria's father.

Aboriginal peoples called Prince Edward Island "Abegweit," derived from a Mi'kmaq word loosely translated as "cradled in the waves." Early French settlers called it Île St- Jean and, when the Treaty of Paris in 1763 gave the island to the British, the name was translated to St. John's Island.

CHARLOTTETOWN

Population (1999)	136,000
Area: Land	5,660 km²
Fresh Water	0 km²
Total	5,660 km²
Capital	Charlottetown
Date of entry into Confederation:	July 1,1873

The island also has several nicknames including the "Million-Acre-Farm" and "The Garden of the Gulf."

History

Although the Mi'kmaq Indians have inhabited the island for the last 2,000 years, there are indications that their ancestors lived there as long as 10,000 years ago. These Aboriginal peoples are said to have reached the island by crossing the low plain now covered by the Northumberland Strait.

In 1534, Jacques Cartier was the first European to set eyes on the island, which he called the "fairest land that may possibly be seen." Despite Cartier's glowing description, settlement of the island was slow. Not until the early 1700s did the French establish a permanent colony and, by 1748, the population was still fewer than 700.

The population of the island grew dramatically following the British expulsion of the Acadians from Nova Scotia in 1755. By the time the French fortress of Louisbourg fell to the British in 1758, the population of the island was more than 5,000. The British forced all but a few hundred of the Acadians to leave the island, even though France did not cede the island until the Treaty of Paris in 1763.

In 1758, the island became part of the British colony of Nova Scotia, which at that time also included the present-day province of New Brunswick. In 1769, the island became a separate colony.

Coat of Arms

Prince Edward Island was plagued throughout most of the colonial period with problems of absentee landowners. Most of the people granted land by the British Crown never set foot on the island. Some refused to sell land to the tenants; others charged outrageous prices to sell, or demanded high rents of those who wished to establish farms on the rich land.

The island's government tried to impose a tax on landowners to cover the cost of administration, but this tax was next to impossible to collect. In 1840, the colony was able to buy land from some of the landlords and make it available for purchase by tenants. Money for this purpose, however, was soon exhausted.

Prince Edward Island hosted the first of the confederation conferences at Charlottetown in 1864. However, the island's leaders dropped out of the confederation discussions after the Quebec City conference later in the same year because they feared the island's autonomy would be jeopardized by joining a large Canadian union.

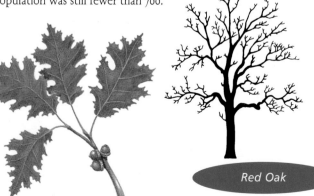

Red Oak

Less than ten years later, that decision was reversed. The debt incurred in building a railway for the island, pressure from the British government, and the attractive promises of the Canadian government compelled Prince Edward Island to join Confederation in 1873. The Canadian promises included an absorption of the debt, year-round communication with the mainland and funds to buy out the absentee landowners.

Coat of Arms

Prince Edward Island's coat of arms, which had been used on the provincial great seal since 1769, was granted officially under King Edward VII in 1905.

The top part of the shield features the English heraldic lion, which appears on the coat of arms of Prince Edward, after whom the province is named, and on the royal coat of arms of King Edward VII, who assigned the provincial arms. The lower part of the shield shows a green island with a large oak tree on the right and three young oaks on the left. The mature tree represents the Oak of England, while the tree saplings represent the province's three counties — King's, Queen's and Prince. The trees rise from a single base, both Britain and P.E.I. being islands.

Motto

PARVA SUB INGENTI
(The small under the protection of the great)

Flag

Prince Edward Island's flag was adopted by an act of legislature in 1964.

The flag is modelled after the coat of arms in rectangular shape and is bordered on the three sides away from the mast by alternate bands of red and white. The flag's proportions are three by length and two by width.

Floral Emblem

Prince Edward Island's floral emblem, the lady's-slipper, was adopted in 1947. The lady's-slipper (Cypripedium acaule) is a species of orchid. It takes its name from the shape of its petals which form a pouch somewhat like a slipper. Bees tumble into the pouch and, in their efforts to scramble out, brush against the male and female flower parts, thus pollinating the flowers. The lady's-slipper grows in shady and moist woodlands and blooms in late May and June.

Lady's -slipper

Other Provincial Symbols

Tartan: Prince Edward Island Tartan

Tree: Red Oak

Bird: Blue Jay

Official Soil: Charlottetown soil

Blue Jay

SASKATCHEWAN

Origin of the Name

The Cree name for the Saskatchewan River was "Kisiskatchewanisipi," meaning "swift-flowing river." Through common use, this eight-syllable name was shortened to Saskatchewan. In 1882, it became the name of one of the districts of the Northwest Territories.

REGINA

Population (1999) 1,026,000
Area: Land ......570,700 km²
  Fresh Water ..81,630 km²
  Total ......652,330 km²
Capital ....Regina
Date of Entry into Confederation:
September 1, 1905

History

Saskatchewan was originally inhabited by Indian tribes of the Athabaskan, Algonquian and Siouan linguistic groups. Three Athabaskan tribes lived in the north: the Chipewyan, the Beaver and the Slavey. Two Algonquian tribes — the Cree and the Blackfoot — occupied the central part of the province. The south was inhabited predominantly by the Siouan tribes — the Assiniboine and the Gros Ventres. The influence of Aboriginal peoples in Saskatchewan is evident from the great variety of Indian place names across the province.

Because the prairie, which makes up much of the province, was of little monetary interest to the early fur traders, southern Saskatchewan was relatively untouched by Europeans for many years. The northern wooded regions, on the other hand, were dotted with fur-trading posts early in Canadian history. The first explorer was Henry Kelsey, an employee of the Hudson's Bay Company, who followed the Saskatchewan River into the plains of Saskatchewan in about 1690.

Both Britain and the Province of Canada sent expeditions in the mid-1800s to explore the area and assess its agricultural potential.

In 1870, the area that now makes up the province of Saskatchewan joined Confederation as part of the Northwest Territories. The *Dominion Lands Act* of 1872, combined with legislation to stimulate immigration, strongly encouraged homesteaders in Saskatchewan. In the 1880s, the newly constructed Canadian Pacific Railway brought settlers to farm the rich land. A great wave of immigration from Eastern Europe swept across the area in the late 19th and early 20th centuries.

In 1905, the Province of Saskatchewan was formed by joining the districts of Saskatchewan and parts of the districts of Athabaska and Assiniboia. It became the only province with boundaries not based on any particular geographical features. Saskatchewan and its neighbouring province of Alberta also share the distinction of being the only Canadian provinces that are not bordered by salt water.

Agriculture, particularly wheat and other cereal crops, but also oilseeds and livestock, continues to be the mainstay of the Saskatchewan economy. The province has 40 percent of Canada's farmland and produces 60 percent of the country's wheat. However, the economy is increasingly diversified thanks to the wealth of mineral resources: Saskatchewan has half the world's potash reserves, Canada's largest heavy oil reserves, coal, gold, and rich uranium deposits. The one million inhabitants of Saskatchewan, about 3.3 percent of Canada's population, reflect the ethnic diversity of Aboriginal, British, German, Ukrainian, Scandinavian, French and other peoples. The largest city is Saskatoon, which has a population of 219,000. Regina, the seat of government, has a population of 193,000.

Coat of Arms

Coat of Arms

Saskatchewan's shield of arms was granted in 1906 under King Edward VII. The crest, supporters and motto were granted in 1986 by Governor General Jeanne Sauvé in the name of Queen Elizabeth II.

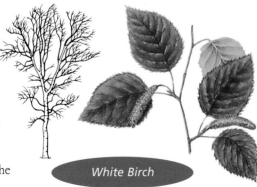
White Birch

Wheat Sheaf

Saskatchewan District Tartan

Saskatchewan Dress Tartan

The top of the shield of arms features a red lion, a traditional royal symbol, on a horizontal gold band; the middle and lower parts of the shield feature three gold wheat sheaves on a green background, symbolizing Saskatchewan's agriculture and resources.

The shield is supported by a royal lion and a white-tailed deer, an animal indigenous to Saskatchewan. Both supporters wear collars of Prairie Indian beadwork. From each collar hangs a badge in the form of the six-pointed star (stylized lily) of the Saskatchewan Order of Merit. The badge worn by the lion displays Canada's emblem, the maple leaf, while the badge worn by the deer displays Saskatchewan's official flower, the western red lily.

Immediately above the shield is a helmet, which represents Saskatchewan's co-sovereign status within Confederation. The helmet is decorated with mantling in Canada's national colours — red and white. Above the helmet is a wreath which supports a beaver — Canada's national animal. The beaver represents the North, the fur trade and the province's native people. The beaver holds a western red lily, the floral emblem of the province. The Crown, a symbol of Saskatchewan's direct link with the Sovereign through the Lieutenant Governor, surmounts the beaver at the top of the coat of arms.

Western Red Lily

Motto

MULTIS E GENTIBUS VIRES
(From many peoples strength)

Flag

Saskatchewan's flag was adopted by the province's legislative assembly and proclaimed by the Lieutenant Governor in 1969. The flag is divided horizontally into two equal parts, one green, the other gold. The green represents the northern forests of the province and the gold symbolizes the southern grain fields. The

Saskatchewan shield of arms is in the upper left quarter of the flag near the staff. The provincial floral emblem, the western red lily, is positioned on the fly half of the flag. The flag is based on a design by Anthony Drake, whose submission was chosen in a provincial design competition. The flag's proportions are two by length and one by width.

Floral Emblem

Saskatchewan's floral emblem, the western red lily, was adopted in 1941. The flower, a protected species, grows in moist meadows and semi-wooded areas. It stands out brilliantly with its flaming red blossoms against a natural green background.

Sharp-Tailed Grouse

Other Provincial Symbols

Tartans: Saskatchewan District Tartan (registered with the Court of the Lord Lyon, King of Arms of Scotland in 1961); and Saskatchewan Dress Tartan (registered in 1997).

Tree: White Birch

Bird: Sharp-tailed Grouse

Plant: Wheat (sheaf)

Mineral: Potash (Sylvite)

Potash

ALBERTA

Origin of the Name

Alberta was named for Queen Victoria's fourth daughter, Princess Louise Caroline Alberta, the wife of the Marquess of Lorne, who was Governor General of Canada in 1882 when the District of Alberta was created as part of the Northwest Territories. In 1905, the name was retained when the District of Alberta was joined with parts of the Districts of Athabasca, Assiniboia and Saskatchewan to create the present-day province of Alberta.

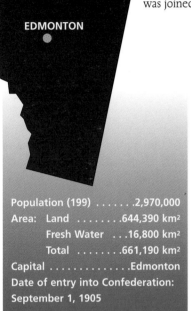

EDMONTON

Population (199)	2,970,000
Area: Land	........644,390 km²
Fresh Water	...16,800 km²
Total	.......661,190 km²
Capital	.............Edmonton

Date of entry into Confederation:
September 1, 1905

History

The oldest identified archaeological sites in Alberta date back approximately 11,000 years. When Europeans reached what is now Alberta in the mid-18th century, the area was home to many different First Nations. Historically, the Blackfoot or Siksika, the Peigan, the Blood or Kainai, the Tsuu T'ina or Sarsi, the Kutenai, the Cree, the Assiniboin or Nakota, the Gros Ventre or Atsina, the Beaver or Tsatinne, the Chipewyan and Slavey or Dene Tha, all had close associations with lands now located within Alberta.

In 1778, fur trader Peter Pond established the first fur trade post within the boundaries of modern Alberta. Soon other posts were constructed on the Athabasca, Peace and North Saskatchewan rivers by both the North West and Hudson's Bay companies. Often, the posts were built virtually side-by-side, as at Fort George and Buckingham House on the North Saskatchewan River or Fort Chipewyan and Nottingham House on Lake Athabasca.

Lodgepole Pine

Competition for furs ended briefly after the North West and Hudson's Bay companies merged in 1821, but by the mid-19th century free traders operating in Alberta reintroduced competition into the fur trade.

In the mid-19th century, several scientific expeditions, most notably Captain John Palliser's expedition of 1857-1860, examined the agricultural potential of the Canadian west. Palliser believed that the southern prairies, sometimes referred to as Palliser's Triangle, were too dry for farming, but further north he and other observers, including the notable naturalist and geologist Henry Youle Hind, thought the land was fertile and well suited to agricultural settlement. In 1869, the British and Canadian governments began negotiations with the Hudson's Bay Company over the transfer of the company's trade monopoly and lands. In 1870, these lands, including most of present-day Alberta, were acquired by the Government of Canada.

Coat of Arms

Settlement was slow until the Canadian Pacific Railway reached Alberta in 1883. The railway made it easier for new settlers to get to Alberta and to sell the crops they grew. In 1891, a railway was completed from Calgary to Strathcona, across the North Saskatchewan River from Edmonton. Other railway lines followed, including the transcontinental Grand Trunk Pacific and Canadian Northern railways, which reached Edmonton in 1911.

In 1905, Alberta and its neighbour, Saskatchewan, entered Confederation. For the first time, Canadian provinces were joined from sea to sea. Settlement boomed in Alberta. Land in the new province was readily available at low cost under the *Homestead Act* or could be purchased from railway and other land companies. The discovery of new strains of wheat and other grains suited to western Canadian growing conditions and new methods of farming also helped encourage rapid settlement.

In 1891, the population of Alberta was about 26,500 people. By 1901, this number had grown to about 73,000. In ten years, the population increased over five times to 374,000 in 1911, before increasing substantially again to more than 584,000 in 1921. As a result, the population of Alberta came to be made up of many peoples of different backgrounds, languages and cultures.

Coat of Arms

Alberta's coat of arms was granted under King Edward VII in 1907. In the name of Queen Elizabeth ll, Governor General Edward Schreyer granted a crest, supporters and motto in 1980 to mark the 75th anniversary of the creation of the province.

The upper portion of the shield displays the St. George's Cross, while a beaver is displayed predominantly in the crest above the shield. The lower part of the shield portrays the varied nature of the province's landscape — mountains, foothills, prairie and grain fields.

At the base of the shield is the province's floral emblem, the wild rose. The shield is supported by a lion and a pronghorned antelope.

Motto

FORTIS ET LIBER
(Strong and free)

Flag

The Alberta flag was first used in 1967 and officially adopted the following year by the provincial legislature. The flag features the Alberta shield of arms in the centre of a royal ultramarine blue background. The flag's proportions are two by length and one by width.

Rocky Mountain Big Horn Sheep

Floral Emblem

The wild rose, also known as the prickly rose, became Alberta's floral emblem in 1930. It is the most widely distributed native rose in Canada, ranging from Quebec to British Columbia. Chosen as the provincial floral emblem by the school children of Alberta, the wild rose is popular for both its colour and fragrance. Its scarlet berries are a valuable source of winter food for birds.

Prickly Rose

Petrified Wood

Other Provincial Symbols

Tartan: Alberta Tartan

Tree: Lodgepole Pine

Bird: Great Horned Owl

Stone: Petrified Wood

Mammal: Rocky Mountain Big Horn Sheep

Fish: Bull Trout

Colours: Blue and Gold

Great Horned Owl

Bull Trout

NEWFOUNDLAND

Origin of the Name

King Henry VII of England referred to the land discovered by John Cabot in 1497 as the "New Found Launde."

History

The aboriginal inhabitants of Newfoundland were the Beothuk Indians. Archaeological evidence suggests that the Beothuk inhabited Newfoundland long before European colonization and that they may have been descended from earlier people who occupied the Island for several thousand years.

ST. JOHN'S

At the time of European contact, the Aboriginal inhabitants of the Island of Newfoundland, the Beothuk, occupied at least the south and northeast coasts of Newfoundland, numbering perhaps no more than 500 to 1000 people. By the early 1800s, disease and conflicts with settlers and others frequenting the island led to their extinction.

Population (1999) 534,000
Area: Land . . . . .371,690 km²
         Fresh Water . . . .34,030 km²
         Total . . . . .405,720 km²
Capital . . . . .St. John's
Date of entry into Confederation:
March 31, 1949

There were, and still are, a relatively large number of Inuit concentrated in the coastal communities of Northern Labrador.

The first Europeans to visit Newfoundland were Norsemen who are thought to have arrived in the 10th century. Other early visitors, the Basques, Portuguese, Spanish, British and French, staged fishing expeditions in the 16th century and possibly earlier.

The Genoese navigator Giovanni Caboto, known as John Cabot, landed on the island on June 24, 1497, on the feast of St. John the Baptist. Cabot called the new land "St. John's Isle" in honour of the saint and claimed it for Henry VII of England, his patron and employer.

Black Spruce

In 1583, Sir Humphrey Gilbert reasserted England's claim to the Island of Newfoundland and the surrounding seas for Queen Elizabeth I.

In 1610, a group of merchants under King James I tried to establish a permanent settlement at what is now Cupids on Conception Bay. This was the first recorded attempt to establish a formal English colony in present-day Canada.

Anglo-French colonial warfare shaped the history of Newfoundland during the 17th and 18th centuries. France, already well-established on the mainland of Eastern Canada, began to make claims to parts of Newfoundland. In 1662, France established a fort and colony at Placentia, despite protests from British merchants and fishermen. The Treaty of Utrecht in 1713 ended a long period of raids and skirmishes by both nations, and reconfirmed British sovereignty over Newfoundland and the fishing banks.

The Seven Years War (1756-63) saw a resumption in hostilities between England and France. However, with the signing of the Treaty of Paris in 1763, British sovereignty was again recognized.

Coat of Arms

In 1832, the people of Newfoundland were granted the right to vote for an elected assembly. However, conflict between the assembly and the appointed council led to the collapse of the colonial government by 1841. In 1847, the British government decided to revert to a separate assembly and council, although the council was not made responsible to the assembly for its actions. After much debate, Newfoundland was finally given responsible government in 1855.

Newfoundland sent observers to the confederation conference in Quebec City in 1864, but postponed its decision on whether or not to join the union. Confederation became the major issue in the general election in Newfoundland in 1869, but the concept did not gain popular approval.

Newfoundland Pony

By 1933, the Great Depression, combined with other factors, brought the Newfoundland government close to bankruptcy. Newfoundland, a Dominion within the Commonwealth, asked the British government to suspend the legislature. A governor and a six-member Commission of Government ruled Newfoundland from 1934 until 1949.

After World War II, the question of Newfoundland's future status became an issue once again. In 1948, it was decided to hold a public referendum on two options: retention of the Commission of Government or a return to the 1934 status as a Dominion within the Commonwealth. However, a vigorous popular movement forced British authorities to include a third referendum option: union with Canada. Following two referenda, Confederation with Canada won with 52 percent of the vote. On March 31, 1949, Newfoundland became the tenth province of Canada.

Coat of Arms

Newfoundland's coat of arms, one of the oldest of any province or territory, was granted by King Charles I in 1637.

In commemoration of Cabot's discovery of the island on the feast of St. John, the shield is divided into four parts by a silver cross similar to the cross on the Arms of the Knights of St. John. Two of the four quarters display lions and two display unicorns. These represent the supporters of the Royal Arms after the union of England and Scotland.

Two Aboriginal men in warlike clothing, representing the island's original inhabitants, support the shield.

The elk in the crest above the shield is included as an example of the fauna of Newfoundland. However, the elk has never been native to the province; it is possible that the animal was meant to be a caribou.

Motto

QUAERITE PRIME REGNUM DEI
(Seek ye first the Kingdom of God)

Atlantic Puffin

Labradorite

Flag

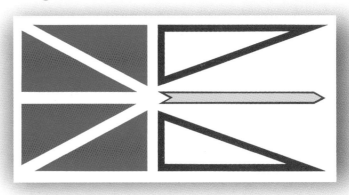

Newfoundland's flag, designed by artist Christopher Pratt, was adopted by the provincial legislature in 1980. Its white area symbolizes snow and ice; blue, the sea; red, human effort; and gold, confidence in the future. The image of the trident (three-pronged spear) on the left side of the flag emphasizes Newfoundland's dependence on fishing and the sea. The two red triangles on the right stand for the mainland and island parts of the province, and the golden arrow represents hope for the future. When the flag is hung as a banner, the arrow assumes the aspect of a sword, a reminder of the sacrifices made in war. The flag's proportions are two by length and one by width.

Floral Emblem

The insect-eating pitcher plant, adopted as Newfoundland's floral emblem in 1954, is the most unusual of Canada's official flowers. It was first chosen as a symbol of Newfoundland by Queen Victoria, to be engraved on the newly-minted Newfoundland penny. It was used on the island's coinage until 1938.

Pitcher Plant

Other Provincial Symbols

Tree: Black Spruce

Bird: Atlantic Puffin

Gemstone: Labradorite

Dog: Newfoundland Dog

Pony: Newfoundland Pony

Newfoundland Dog

Origin of the Name

Most of the Northwest Territories was known as the North-Western Territory until 1870. Then as now, the name is primarily descriptive of the location of the Territories.

History

The Northwest Territories were inhabited by Inuit and Indian tribes long before the Europeans arrived in search of the elusive Northwest Passage. Native Inuit included the Mackenzie, Copper, Caribou and Central tribes. There were also many Indian tribes when the Europeans first arrived, among them the Yellow-Knife, Chipewyan, Sekani, Beaver, Nahanni, Dogrib and Slavey. Some Indian tribes in the area spoke a form of the Athabaskan language, the only native language in North America to have traces of an Asiatic origin.

The first European explorers were the Vikings, who sailed to the eastern Arctic in about 1000 A.D. However, Martin Frobisher's expeditions in the 1570s were the first recorded visits to the Northwest Territories by an explorer. In 1610, Henry Hudson, while looking for the Northwest Passage, landed briefly on the western shore of the bay that bears his name. His discovery opened the interior of the continent to further exploration.

YELLOWKNIFE

Population 40,500 (1999)
Total Area: . . . . . . .1,171,918 km²
Capital . . . . .Yellowknife
Date of creation of territory:
July 15, 1870

By the 1700s, the Northwest Territories were dominated by two fur-trading companies: the Hudson's Bay Company, based in London, England, and the North West Company based in Montreal.

In 1870, the British government transferred control of the North-Western Territory to Canada, and the Hudson's Bay Company sold Rupert's Land to the new Dominion for 300,000 pounds sterling. The combined area was renamed the Northwest Territories. Ten years later the British government annexed the islands of the Arctic archipelago to these territories.

At some time in their history, the Northwest Territories have included all of Alberta, Saskatchewan, Yukon, and most of Manitoba, Ontario and Quebec.

In 1870, the original tiny province of Manitoba was carved out of the area. In 1905, both Alberta and Saskatchewan were created from the Territories. Manitoba was increased in size in 1881 by taking land from the Territories. In 1898, Yukon became a separate territory, while the provinces of Manitoba, Ontario and Quebec were enlarged by taking land from the Territories in 1912. Even with this loss of land, the Northwest Territories remained Canada's largest political subdivision (with just over a third of the country's total area) until 1999.

In April 1999, the Northwest Territories were divided in two, with 60 percent of the land being transferred to the new territory of Nunavut in Canada's eastern Arctic.

Coat of Arms

The Northwest Territories coat of arms was granted by Queen Elizabeth II in 1956. The white upper third of the shield represents the polar icepack and is crossed by a wavy blue line that symbolizes the Northwest Passage. The lower portion is divided diagonally by a wavy line which represents the treeline; the green stands for the forested areas south of the treeline, and the red represents the tundra to the north.

Coat of Arms

Jack Pine

Minerals and fur, the foundation of northern wealth, are represented by gold billets in the green section of the shield and the mask of a white fox in the red section. The crest is supported by two narwhals; the compass rose between them represents the North Pole.

Other Territorial Symbols

Tartan: Northwest Territories Tartan

Tree: Jack Pine

Bird: Gyrfalcon

Mineral: Native Gold

Flag

The flag of the Northwest Territories was adopted by the territorial council in 1969 following a nationwide design competition won by Robert Bessant of Margaret, Manitoba. The blue panels at either end of the flag represent the lakes and waters of the Territories. The white centre panel symbolizes the ice and snow of the North and contains the shield of the territorial coat of arms. The flag's proportions are four by length and two by width.

Floral Emblem

The Northwest Territories' floral emblem, the mountain avens, was adopted in 1957. The mountain avens is a member of the rose family, and grows in the Eastern and Central Arctic on high, barren rocky ground. It has narrow basal leaves, and supports a single white flower on a short stem.

Gyrfalcon

Mountain Avens

Native Gold

YUKON

Origin of the Name

The territory's name comes from the native name word "Yu-kun-ah" meaning great river. In 1846, chief trader John Bell of the Hudson's Bay Company canoed down the Porcupine River to its confluence with the Yukon River, where he met natives who told him that the name of the big river was the "youcon". The Yukon River is the fifth longest in North America.

WHITEHORSE

Population (1999): 31,500
Area: Land . . . . .478,970 km²
    Fresh Water . . . . .4,480 km²
    Total . . . . . . .483,450 km²
Capital . . . . .Whitehorse
Date of creation of territory:
June 13, 1898

History

Yukon was probably the first area in Canada to be settled, following the migration of the ancestors of First Nations people across the Bering Strait land bridge from Asia to North America some 4,000 years ago. Language is central to Yukon First Nation heritage. The history and traditions of the many Yukon First Nations have been passed down through the generations orally by the teachings of elders. There are seven Athapaskan languages spoken in Yukon: Gwich'in, Han, Kaska, Tagish, Upper Tanana, Northern and Southern Tutchone. Tlingit is also spoken in southwestern Yukon.

In 1825, John Franklin became the first European to reach Yukon, then part of Rupert's Land, when he followed the Arctic coastline in search of the Northwest Passage. By 1848, the Hudson's Bay Company had established four trading posts on a traditional First Nation trading route.

In 1870, the Government of Canada acquired the territory from the Hudson's Bay Company and the entire region became known as the Northwest Territories. The boundaries of Yukon were first drawn in 1895, when it became a district of the Northwest Territories. Because of its remote location and severe climate, Yukon's population remained sparse until the discovery of gold.

After gold was discovered at Rabbit Creek (later renamed Bonanza Creek) in 1896, the Klondike became one of the most populated regions in the northwestern part of the continent as thousands of hopeful goldseekers headed north. By 1898-99, Dawson City, at the junction of the Klondike and Yukon rivers, was home to 40,000 people.

The sudden increase in population during the Klondike Gold Rush prompted the federal government to exert stronger control in Yukon. It became a separate territory in 1898 with passage of the *Yukon Act*. Dawson was chosen as the new territory's capital city.

Between 1896 and 1903, more than $95 million in gold were mined from the Klondike region. But once the easily extracted placer gold was depleted the population dropped to 8,512 by 1911. Today, Dawson's population is approximately 1,200. However, the Klondike is still a major tourist attraction in Yukon. August 17, "Discovery Day", is an annual holiday celebrating the anniversary of the initial discovery of gold at Bonanza Creek.

When Yukon became a separate territory, the *Yukon Act* of 1898 provided for a Commissioner and a legislative council of six, all appointed by the Government of Canada. In subsequent years, elected officials were included on the council; the first wholly-elected council was elected in 1909.

In 1979, an Executive Committee was established to assist the Territorial Commissioner in the executive function, and the elected members of the Executive Committee or Council have progressively assumed greater responsibilities. With the formal introduction of party politics in 1978, the elected leader of the majority party in the legislature became known as the Government Leader. When responsible government was established in 1979, the Commissioner no longer participated in the Executive Council. The Government Leader has the authority to determine the size and the appointments to the Executive Council, paralleling the function of the premiers in the provinces.

Coat of Arms

The Yukon coat of arms was granted by Queen Elizabeth II and adopted by the Yukon Legislative Council in 1956. The Cross of St. George at the top of the shield refers to

Coat of Arms

the early explorers and fur traders from England, while the round panel of heraldic fur in the centre of the cross symbolizes the fur trade. The wavy white and blue vertical stripes in the lower part of the shield represent the Yukon River and gold-bearing creeks of the Klondike. The red spire-like forms represent the mountains of Yukon, and the two gold discs in each spire symbolize the territory's mineral resources. The crest above the shield features a malamute (or husky) dog standing on a mound of snow.

Other Territorial Symbols

Tartan: Yukon Tartan

Bird: Raven

Gemstone: Lazulite

Flag

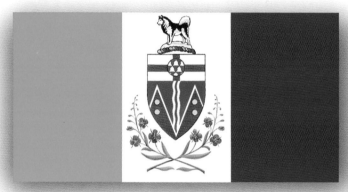

The Yukon flag was adopted by the Territorial Council in 1967.

The flag is made up of three vertical panels. The green panel on the staff side symbolizes the forests, the white in the centre represents the snow, while the deep blue on the fly side represents the Yukon's rivers and lakes. The centre panel features the territorial coat of arms and floral emblem, the fireweed. The flag was designed by Lynn Lambert, a student from Haines Junction, Yukon, who won the territorial flag-designing competition during Canada's centennial year. The flag's proportions are two by length and one by width.

Raven

Floral Emblem

The Yukon's floral emblem, the fireweed ("epilobium augustifolium"), was adopted in 1957. The hardy magenta fireweed blooms along roadsides, river bars and clearings from mid-July to September. It is one of the first plants to appear in burned areas.

Fireweed

Lazulite

43

NUNAVUT

Origin of the Name

Nunavut means "our land" in the Inuit language of Inuktitut

History

The earliest traces of settlement in Canada's Arctic date back some 4,000 years, when the first of a number of hunting societies traveled across the Bering Strait into northern Canada. The Inuit, who make up 85 percent of Nunavut's

IQALUIT

> Population (1999): 27,000
> Total Area: ....1,994, 000 km²
> Capital ....Iqaluit
> Date of creation of the territory:
> April 1, 1999

population, are descended from one of these societies, the Thule, whose presence dates back at least 1,000 years.

The first European contact with the Inuit came with the arrival of the Norsemen in the 11th century. They were followed by explorers in search of the Northwest Passage — first in Elizabethan times and, again, in the 19th century. Later came whalers, Hudson's Bay Company traders, missionaries and the Royal Canadian Mounted Police.

The idea of dividing the Northwest Territories in two was first raised during the government of John Diefenbaker in the early 1960s. The government went as far as introducing a bill in the House of Commons to divide the Northwest Territories. The bill was allowed to die on the order paper after some residents of the eastern Arctic flew down to Ottawa and told a House of Commons Committee that the people of the north had not been consulted on the matter.

The Government appointed a three-man commission to examine political development in the Canadian Arctic and to make recommendations to Parliament. The Carrothers Commission held some hearings in the north and recommended that the issue of dividing the Northwest Territories be further examined in ten years time.

In 1971, the leadership of the newly created Inuit Tapirisat of Canada stated their objective of creating a new territory for the Inuit in the eastern Arctic. They insisted that it had to be part of any final land claims agreement, in spite of objections from both the Northwest Territories government in Yellowknife and the federal government. They were successful in persuading the Northwest Territories Legislative Assembly to put the issue to public debate.

The first major test for Nunavut came in the plebiscite of 1982 in which all residents of the Northwest Territories were asked to vote on the issue of division. Proponents of division won the plebiscite 53 percent to 47 percent. Ten years of negotiations on a boundary for the new territory were followed by another plebiscite in 1992 to ratify the boundary. The Government of Canada then agreed to include the creation of Nunavut as part of the final land claims agreement which recognized Inuit ownership of 350,000 square kilometres of land. The *Nunavut Act* was passed by Parliament in 1993 and came into effect on April 1, 1999.

Coat of Arms

Nunavut accounts for roughly 20 percent of Canada's land mass, making it the country's largest political subdivision. The territory is governed by a 19-member legislative assembly which operates consensus-style without political parties. Nunavut's largest employer is the government. Other important economic sectors include mining, construction, tourism and traditional activities such as hunting, trapping, fishing and arts and crafts.

Coat of Arms

The Nunavut coat of arms was granted by Governor General Roméo LeBlanc on April 1, 1999. The colours blue and gold symbolize the riches of the land, sea and sky. In the base of the shield, the inuksuk symbolizes the stone monuments which guide the people on the land and mark sacred and other special places. The qulliq, or Inuit stone lamp, represents the light and warmth of family and community.

Above, the concave arc of five gold circles refers to the life-giving properties of the sun arching above and below the horizon, the unique part of the Nunavut year. The star is the Niqirtsituq, the North Star, the traditional guide for navigation. More broadly, the star represents the unchanging nature of the leadership of elders in the community.

In the crest, the iglu represents the traditional life of the people and the means of survival. It also symbolizes the assembled members of the legislature meeting together for the good of Nunavut. The Royal Crown symbolizes public government for all the people of Nunavut and the equivalent status of Nunavut with other territories and provinces in Canadian Confederation.

The tuktu (caribou) and qilalugaq tugaalik (narwhal) refer to land and sea animals which are part of the rich natural heritage of Nunavut and provide sustenance for its people. The compartment at the base is composed of land and sea and features three important species of Arctic wild flowers.

Motto

The motto, in Inuktitut ᓄᓇᕗᑦ ᓴᖏᓂᕗᑦ or
NUNAVUT SANGINIVUT
in Latin, means "Nunavut our strength".

Flag

The flag of Nunavut, granted by Governor General Roméo LeBlanc on April 1, 1999, features the colours white, blue and gold, which symbolize the riches of the land, sea and sky. Red is a reference to Canada.

The inuksuk symbolizes the stone monuments which guide the people on the land and mark sacred and other special places.

The star is the Niqirtsituq, the North Star, the traditional guide for navigation. More broadly, the star represents the unchanging nature of the leadership of elders in the community.

The Order of Canada

The Order of Canada — our country's highest honour for lifetime achievement — was instituted on July 1, 1967, the 100th anniversary of Confederation. From local citizens to national and international personalities, all Canadians are eligible for the Order of Canada, which is conferred in recognition of outstanding achievement and lifetime contribution in all major fields of endeavour. Appointments are made by the Governor General, based on the recommendations of the Advisory Council of the Order, which meets twice a year under the chairmanship of the Chief Justice of Canada to consider nominations submitted by members of the public.

There are three levels of membership: the Companion level, recognizing the highest degree of service to Canada or humanity; the Officer level, recognizing national service and merit of a high degree; and the Member level, recognizing outstanding contributions at the local or regional level or in a specialized field of activity. The number of living Companions is limited by the constitution to 165; Companions may be appointed only when a vacancy occurs, while recipients of the Officer or Member level may be upgraded.

Companion

Officer

Member

The Order of Canada's badge is in the form of a stylized, six-pointed snowflake bearing the Crown and a maple leaf. It is worn at the neck by Companions and Officers and on the left breast by Members. Recipients are entitled to place the initials of their level of appointment to the Order after their names: C.M., O.C., or C.C., and all may wear a small replica of the badge on street clothes. The motto of the Order of Canada is DESIDERANTES MELIOREM PATRIAM, meaning "they desire a better country."

The Order of Ontario

In 1986, the Government of Ontario established the Order of Ontario, which is awarded annually to Ontario residents who have demonstrated excellence and achievement of the highest degree in any field of endeavour and whose contributions have enriched the lives of their fellow man and contributed to the betterment of their

communities. All nominations for the Order are considered by an Advisory Council comprising the Chief Justice of Ontario, who is Chairperson, the Speaker of the Legislative Assembly of Ontario, and the Secretary of the Cabinet and Clerk of the Executive Council. The Lieutenant Governor is the Honorary Chairperson of the Advisory Council.

The insignia of the Order is a stylized trillium, Ontario's floral emblem, in white and green enamel, edged in gold. In the centre of the trillium is the shield of arms of the province, surmounted by the Crown. The ribbons of the Order are red, the colour of the flag of Ontario, and white, green and gold, the colours of the trillium.

The National Order of Quebec

In 1984, the Quebec Legislature created the National Order of Quebec to honour individuals who have helped gain recognition and outreach for Quebec. Whether in the scientific, artistic or social spheres, the National Order bears witness to their accomplishments. The Order's motto is "Honour to the people of Quebec." In fact, the government honours individuals nominated by public appeal in the name of the Quebec population.

The insignia of the National Order of Quebec is awarded annually by the premier of Quebec on the favorable advice of a special nine-member elected Council. There are three levels of decoration in the Order: Grand Officer, Officer and Knight. The members of the Order are authorized to use the initials corresponding to their level: Grand Officer (G.O.Q.), Officer (O.Q.), or Knight (K.O.Q.).

The National Order can be awarded to foreign personalities in accordance with the *National Order of Quebec Act* (L.R.Q., c. 07-.01) and can even be given posthumously.

The Order of British Columbia

The Order of British Columbia was created by the provincial legislature in 1989 to recognize those persons who have served with the greatest distinction and excelled in any field of endeavour benefiting the people of British Columbia or elsewhere. The honour is conferred annually by the Lieutenant Governor, based on the recommendations of a seven-member advisory council, chaired by the provincial Chief Justice. The Lieutenant Governor is Honorary Chairperson of the Advisory Council. Members of the Order may use the initials O.B.C. after their names. The insignia of the Order of British Columbia is the visible mark of its honour and is in the form of a medal. The medal is a stylistic dogwood (British Columbia's floral emblem), featuring a crowned shield of arms. The recipient may wear a full-size medal of the Order suspended from a ribbon which passes around the neck. A lapel pin button of the Order may also be worn.

The Order of Prince Edward Island

The Order of Prince Edward Island, the province's highest honour, is awarded to individual islanders whose efforts and accomplishments have been truly exemplary. The Order was created in 1996 and formalized by the provincial legislature in 1997 to encourage and acknowledge outstanding achievements and contributions of individual citizens to the social, cultural and economic life of the province and its residents.

An independent Advisory Council considers nominations for the Order and makes final recommendations to the Premier as President of the Executive Council. The Lieutenant Governor, who is Chancellor of the Order of Prince Edward Island, confers the honour on not more than three people at an annual ceremony at Government House. The Order's insignia include an impressive enameled medallion (Medal of Merit), which incorporates the provincial emblem against a background of gold and blue, as well as a stylized lapel pin and a miniature medal, to be worn on less formal occasions. Recipients are entitled to use the letters O.P.E.I. after their names.

The Saskatchewan Order of Merit

The Saskatchewan Order of Merit, the province's most prestigious honour, was established in 1985 to recognize individual excellence, outstanding achievement and exceptional contributions to the social, cultural and economic well-being of the province and its residents. The Order is awarded to a maximum of ten individuals annually by the Lieutenant Governor, based on the recommendations of the Saskatchewan Honours Advisory Council.

The Order recognizes Saskatchewan residents who have made their mark in such areas as the arts, agriculture, business and industry, community leadership, the occupations or professions, public service, research, and volunteer service.

The insignia worn by members of the Saskatchewan Order of Merit include a silver and enamel medal representing a stylized western red lily (the provincial floral emblem), bearing the Crown and shield of arms of the province, and suspended from a ribbon of green and gold — the province's official colours. There is also a lapel pin representing a stylized lily and bearing the Crown. Recipients of the Order are entitled to use the letters S.O.M. after their names.

The Alberta Order of Excellence

The Alberta Order of Excellence was established in 1979 to recognize individuals who have rendered service of the greatest distinction, and of singular excellence for, or on behalf of, Albertans. The Order of Excellence is the highest honour that can be bestowed on an Albertan by the Province. The Lieutenant Governor of Alberta is Chancellor of the Order. The Council of the Alberta Order of Excellence, a volunteer body of six prominent Albertans, makes recommendation to the Lieutenant Governor as to which individuals should be honoured with membership in the Order.

The Order's insignia consists of a silver, gilt and enamel medallion attached to a ribbon distinctive to the province, which is presented to Members along with a miniature of the insignia design. The gold detail on the four arms of the medallion represents prairie wheat. Roses portray the floral emblem of Alberta, while the central circle contains the provincial Coat of Arms. Members of the Order are entitled to use the initials A.O.E. after their names.

Suggestions for
Classroom Activities

The activity pages in this section have been designed to assist teachers in developing classroom programs based on the theme of Canadian citizenship. Teachers are encouraged to have the activity pages colour-photocopied and distributed to students to foster classroom participation.

The following teaching ideas are intended as starting points for classroom activities. Teachers will want to adapt and modify these learning tools to meet the needs of their classes.

There are endless possibilities for student participation. For example, a quiz could be developed using information from the national, provincial and territorial pages. Classes could also participate in historical role playing. Some students could be assigned to represent provinces or territories already in Confederation while others could represent British North American colonies contemplating union with Canada. The resulting debate could lead to a greater understanding of our historical past as well as an appreciation of our evolution into nationhood and what it means to be a Canadian citizen.

 ## Getting Started

Use the *Symbols around us* page to draw students' attention to everyday symbols that they encounter. Have students begin a symbol search using the newspaper, yellow pages, school, home, community and other sources that could spark a sense of adventure. Present the enclosed Symbols Chart poster to your class. Discuss the various Canadian symbols, pictorial representations and other material contained in the poster.

 ## Canadian Flags

Use the *Canadian flags* page to identify the flags shown and discuss the story that each one tells. Have students note where they see flags flying in their community. Assign students different provinces and territories and ask them to write an imaginative story of the life of a young person in that area of the country.

 ## Coats of Arms

Discuss the meaning of the coats of arms presented on the *Coats of arms* page. Translate Canada's motto (A MARI USQUE AD MARE) into as many languages as possible.

Have students use the *Creating your personal coat of arms* page to tap their creativity in drawing a personal coat of arms.

 ## Emblems of Canada

Give students two or three overnight homework opportunities to find as many Canadian flags as they can. Note product labels inside people's shirts, "Made in Canada" tags in stores, stickers on book spines, blue pages in the phone book, flags on and in public buildings, and anything produced by the Government of Canada, as possible locations. Have a discussion about why the flag is an important identifier.

 ## Floral Emblems

Use the *Floral emblems* page to identify the floral emblems shown and to discuss the location and characteristics of each one.

Research the wildflowers growing near your school or at a local conservation area.

Plant flowers and trees around the school that symbolize the importance of the environment.

 ## Stamps of Canada

Use the *Stamps of Canada* page as a springboard for the study of Canadian stamps.

Student stamp collectors might enjoy presenting their collections to the class.

 ## Canadian Heroes

Ask students to think about what makes someone a hero. Then ask them to identify some Canadian heroes. These heroes can be individuals such as prime ministers or athletes, or groups of people such as peacekeepers, war veterans, artists or scientists. Why do students admire these people? What characteristics do students think they share with their heroes?

Organize a Canadian hero quiz for students. Here are a few examples to get you started:

Q. Who was the first Canadian woman is space?
A. Roberta Bondar.
Q. Can you name the two Canadians who discovered insulin?
A. Banting and Best.
Q. Who was the Canadian engineer who invented Standard Time and the time zones?
A. Sir Sandford Fleming.
Q. Name the young Canadian who raised money for cancer with his "Marathon of Hope"
A. Terry Fox.

 ## Supplemental Activities

Encourage students to write a *What Canada Means To Me* essay and to investigate the schedule of events for upcoming holiday celebrations in the community. Write out the words to *O Canada* and have the students copy them down to foster memorization and a discussion of their meaning.

A year-end Canada Day assembly could involve displays of students' work and class projects, choral readings, a guest speaker (local politician), Canadian folk songs, a Canada cake prepared by students, slides brought in by students from trips taken to different parts of Canada, and special Canada Day messages.

Symbols around us

We see symbols all around us every day. Symbols communicate a message to us in picture form.

1. Can you identify each symbol below?

2. Where have you seen each one?

3. Why is each one so important to us?

4. Make a list of some other symbols you have seen. Compare lists with your friends and discuss them.

5. Make up a symbol that you think should be used and explain why.

Canadian flags

Every province and territory in Canada has its own flag. However, the one symbol that unites us all is the red and white national flag of Canada, first raised on February 15, 1965.

1. Label each flag below with the name of the province or territory to which it belongs.

2. Study the flags carefully. Do you see any features that are the same?

3. What story does each flag tell?

4. Make a list of all the different places in your community where the Canadian flag is flown.

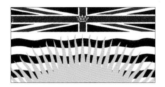

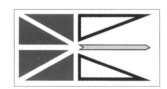

Coats of Arms

Coats of arms first appeared during the Middle Ages when they were painted on shields and banners to identify knights fighting in battles and tournaments. Today, coats of arms are symbols used by countries to identify themselves and to tell the story of their people.

1. Write the name of the Canadian province or territory to which each shield below belongs.

2. Study the shields carefully. Do you see any features that are the same?

3. What story does each shield tell?

4. The Canadian coat of arms is the only symbol that appears on every denomination of Canadian paper money. Look around. Can you find the coat of arms anywhere else?

Creating your
Personal Coat of Arms

In Canada, coats of arms are granted by the Governor General to cities, towns, schools, universities, hospitals, churches, private companies, individuals, cultural organizations and others. They are symbols of authority, ownership and identity and are part of the national honours system. Designed by heralds in the Governor General's office, coats of arms are simple yet colourful, and filled with symbols that have great meaning for their owners.

While coats of arms are different for every individual and organization, they all have one thing in common: they help tell the story of the people they represent.

You can tell your own story by creating a personal coat of arms on the shield on this page. Start by choosing symbols that mean something to you. These symbols can be from nature or they can be invented by people. They can include everything from maple leaves and flowers to ships and musical instruments, but the best coats of arms include only a few items and colours.

The rules of heraldry

As you create your coat of arms, be sure to follow the basic rules of heraldry. The most important rule has to do with colour. Five main colours can be used on a coat of arms: red, blue, green, purple and black. A coat of arms can also feature two metals: silver (shown as white) and gold (shown as yellow). To create a greater contrast between colours, you should draw in your shield with one of the five main colours and then place one of the metal colours (white or gold) on top, or vice versa. To indicate family ties, you may also divide the shield in half horizontally or vertically, colouring one side in a main colour and the other in a metal colour, with the symbols on each side drawn in a colour that contrasts with the background. Other divisions are also possible: check out books on heraldry at your local library to see examples.

You can place additional symbols on your coat of arms by adding a crest above the shield. Can you think of a personal motto for your coat of arms?

When you are finished, share your coat of arms with a friend. Compare notes as to what you have learned. Now that you have made a coat of arms for yourself, you might like to design one for your class or school. Put it up for others to see!

Floral emblems

Each province and territory has adopted a special flower as a symbol of its own part of Canada. The floral emblem of each province and territory is listed below.

1. Show the location of each floral emblem by putting the number beside each one in the correct circle on the map.

2. Canada does not have a national floral emblem. If you could pick one flower to represent our country, which one would it be? Why?

3. Of all the flowers you know, which one would you choose as your own floral emblem? Why?

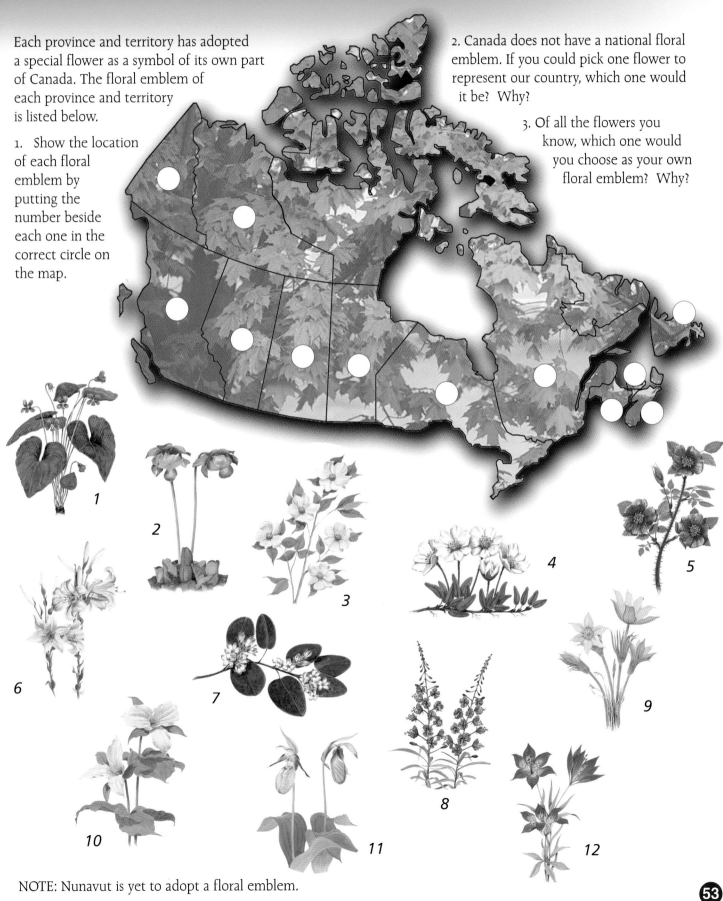

1

2

3

4

5

6

7

8

9

10

11

12

NOTE: Nunavut is yet to adopt a floral emblem.

Stamps of Canada

Canadian postage stamps tell the story of our country. You can discover a great deal about Canadian people and events by studying the words, pictures and symbols on our stamps.

The National
Flag of Canada

Her Majesty
Queen Elizabeth II

1. *What is the most obvious Canadian symbol on this stamp?*

2. *What does VR stand for? What does this tell you about the age of the stamp?*

This 50¢ Bluenose stamp was issued in 1929. The Bluenose was built in Nova Scotia, and has been called the greatest racing schooner of all time.

1. *The Bluenose is a Canadian symbol that appears on one of our coins. Which one?*

2. *Can you spot another Canadian symbol in the top corners of this stamp?*

1. *What police force is shown on this stamp?*

2. *Make up a story about an average day for the Mountie and his horse.*

Create your own Canadian stamp in this space. You might like to use Canadian symbols in your design, or put your own ideas to work.

Stamps reproduced courtesy of Canada Post Corporation.

Coins

Canada did not have its own coins until the mid-1800s. Prior to this, coins from France, Great Britain, Spain, Spanish America, Portugal, and the United States were used.

1. Name each coin. What symbol appears on each?

2. How much would you have if you had one of each coin?

3. Whose picture is on the front of each coin? Why?

Think of a new design for a Canadian coin. Share your design with a friend.

WHERE TO WRITE FOR ADDITIONAL INFORMATION

On the Crown in Canada and to obtain poster-size photographs of The Queen and the Governor General, suitable for framing:

Information Services Directorate
Rideau Hall
1 Sussex Drive
Ottawa ON K1A 0A1
Tel: (613) 993-8200
Web site: http://www.gc.ca

On heraldry:

Canadian Heraldic Authority
Rideau Hall
1 Sussex Drive
Ottawa ON K1A 0A1
Tel: (613) 991-2228
Fax: (613) 990-5818
e-mail: rwatt@gg.ca

On national symbols:

Ceremonial and Canadian Symbols Promotion
Canadian Identity Directorate
Department of Canadian Heritage (15-7-H)
Ottawa ON K1A 0M5
Tel: (819) 994-1616
Web site:
http://www.pch.gc.ca/ceremonial-symb
e-mail: Cérémonial et symboles Ceremonial and Symbols/HullOttawa/PCH/CA

For further information on the provinces and territories, please contact the following addresses appearing below respective provincial/territorial flags

Ontario Travel
Queen's Park
Toronto ON M7A 2E5
Tel: (416) 314-0956
English: 1-800-668-2746
or French: 1-800-268-3736

Communication-Québec
4th floor
1056 Louis Alexandre Taschereau Street
Québec QC G1R 5E6
Tel: (418) 643-1430

Supervisor of Public Inquiries
Nova Scotia Information Service
P.O. Box 608
Halifax NS B3J 2R7
Tel: (902) 424-5200

Service New Brunswick
Unit #3, 410 William Street
Dalhousie NB E8C 2X4
Tel: (506) 453-2525

Travel Manitoba
7th floor - 155 Carlton Street
Winnipeg MB R3C 3H8
Tel: (204) 945-3777
Toll free: 1-800-665-0040

Government of British Columbia
Protocol and Events Branch
P.O. Box 9422
Stn. Prov. Govt.
Victoria BC V8W 9V1
Tel: (250) 387-1616

Island Information Service
P.O. Box 2000
Charlottetown PE C1A 7N8
Tel: (902) 368-4000

Protocol Office
10th Floor, 1919 Saskatchewan Drive
Regina SK S4P 3V7
Tel: (306) 787-3001
Web site: http://www.gov.sk.ca/govt./IGAA

Department of Tourism
15th Floor, 10025 Jasper Avenue
Edmonton AB T5J 3Z3
Tel: (780) 427-4321
Toll free: 1-800-661-8888

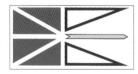

Department of Development and Tourism
Tourism Branch
P.O. Box 8730
St. John's NF A1B 4K2
Tel: (709) 729-2830
1-800-563-6353

Department of Education, Culture and
   Employment
Government of Northwest Territories
P.O. Box 1320
Yellowknife NT X1A 2L9
Tel: (867) 669-2200
1-800-661-0784

Inquiry Centre
Executive Council Office
Government of Yukon
P.O. Box 2703
Whitehorse YT Y1A 2C6
Tel: (867) 667-5811 or 667-5812

Executive and Intergovernmental Affairs
Communications Department
P.O. BAG 800
Iqaluit NT X0A 0H0
Tel: (867) 979-4802

NOTES

DISCOUNTS FOR
NON-COMMERCIAL CUSTOMERS

If your organization would like to purchase large quantities of a publication, you can take advantage of our bulk discounts.

Criteria for bulk discounts

Your bulk purchase must consist of a single title (monograph, or a single issue of a periodical). You are able to include French copies of the same title in your count for discount purposes. For example, if you purchase 50 copies of a book in English and 50 copies of the same book in French, you would be entitled to receive a 25% discount on your whole order.

Some publications (generally flyers or leaflets) come pre-packaged in quantities of 10, 25, 50 or 100. For discount purposes, each of these packages is counted as one (1). For example, to receive a 20% discount on a publication pre-packaged in quantities of 50, you would have to purchase at least 25 packages.

Your order is shipped to a single address. Shipping and handling charges are extra. *Orders from outside Canada must be prepaid. VISA, MasterCard, cheques or international money orders payable to the "Receiver General for Canada" are acceptable.*

If your order meets these criteria, the following scale of discounts will apply:

Quantity	Discount
25–99	20%
100–249	25%
250–499	30%
500–999	35%
1000+	40%

Please note that

(1) there are no returns on bulk orders and

(2) this offer is available only on copies purchased directly from the publisher.

TO ORDER

To order The Symbols of Canada, please indicate the catalogue number: S2-211-1999E Price: $9.95

MAIL TO:
Canadian Government Publishing
Public Works and Government
Services Canada
Ottawa, ON Canada, K1A 0S9

TELEPHONE:
1-800-635-7943 / (819) 956-4800

FAX: 1-800-565-7757 / (819) 994-1498

E-MAIL: publications@pwgsc.gc.ca

WEB SITE: http://publications.gc.ca

CANADIAN GOVERNMENT PUBLISHING
OCTOBER 1999

ORDER FORM
CANADIAN GOVERNMENT PUBLISHING

Name:_____

Company/Department:_____

Address:_____

City:_____ Province:_____ Postal Code:_____ Country:_____

Telephone:_____ Fax:_____ Email:_____

Customer Number (for existing CGP customers): _____

PAYMENT METHOD	
CANADIAN FEDERAL GOVERNMENT DEPARTMENTS AND AGENCIES (EXCL. CROWN CORPORATIONS)	**ALL OTHER CUSTOMERS** (PLEASE CHECK ONE PAYMENT METHOD)
Purchase Order #:_____	☐ Purchase Order #:_____
Department #:_____	☐ Cheque or Money Order enclosed **(payable to the Receiver General for Canada)**
IS Organization Code:_____	
IS Reference Code:_____	☐ Visa ☐ Mastercard
Responsibility Centre Code (if you are part of PWGSC):_____	Credit Card #:_____
	Expiry Date:_____
Note: We cannot process your order without the above information.	Signature:_____

HOW TO ORDER:

Mail to: Canadian Government Publishing
Public Works and Government
Services Canada
Ottawa, ON, Canada, K1A 0S9

Telephone: 1-800-635-7943 / (819) 956-4800
Fax: 1-800-565-7757 / (819) 994-1498
Email: publications@pwgsc.gc.ca
Web site: http://publications.pwgsc.gc.ca

CATALOGUE #	TITLE	QTY.	PRICE	TOTAL

• Prices are subject to change without notice.

• All sales final.

• CGP publications are also available at your local bookstore.

SHIPPING AND HANDLING:

ORDER VALUE	FEE
Under $5	$2.25
$5.01 to $25	$3.50
$25.01 to $75	$5.40
$75.01 to $200	$10.50
over $200	6% of total order value

SUB-TOTAL (ORDER VALUE)	
SHIPPING AND HANDLING	
SUB-TOTAL	
GST 7% (not applicable to Cdn. govt. or international customers)	
TOTAL	